Passion

or

Compassion

by

Antonio Dell'Orco

Cover and interior photos are from Cronaca Della Grande Guerra 1915-1918, © 1992 Edizioni Gino Rossato, Valdagno, Italy.
Cover and interior drawings by Antonio Dell'Orco
Text ©2012 by Antonio Dell'Orco
1. Cataloging in Publication data
2. Dell'Orco, Antonio
3. Passion or Compassion
4. p. cm.
5. ISBN 978-0-9755471-6-8

✝ Divine Mercy Press ✝
3216 Mission Avenue, Suite 138, Oceanside, California, 92058
5319 Willis Avenue, Dallas, Texas 75206
divinemercy@hypersurf.com
http//www.divinemercypress.com

Passion

or

Compassion

by

Antonio Dell'Orco

✠ Divine Mercy Press ✠
Oceanside, California
Dallas, Texas

**Grateful thanks to Pam Pousson
for her help in editing this book.**

Chapter One

At some time in our lives, everyone, no matter who we are or where we come from, will hear the call of home. I had left my home over 50 years ago, to seek my fortune, with others from all over the world, in a land that rewarded hard work and dreams. America has been good to me, and the years have just passed in a blink of an eye. I was always so busy with my work and my family that the years just somehow seemed to slip away. To be sure there had been many cards and letters, and the occasional phone call on birthdays and holidays. I had always thought to return for a visit, planning my trip at some vague point of time in the future. There would always be time, there would always be tomorrow, but suddenly time was up and tomorrow was gone.

I marveled as I sat here in the early morning sun, on a rock I used to climb up to when I was a child. Yesterday I was in California, today as I breathed in the air of home, and took in the beauty of Lake Lake Braies, it was suddenly 50 years ago, and I was saying good-bye. I couldn't have dreamed that it would take me so many years to return. It was just as I remembered it, with the little town I grew up in, that hugged the shores of the lake that shared its name. There was the Storybook Castle with its breathtaking grounds on the other side of the lake, and a large hospital that gleamed in the morning light. It always surprised me that there was such a fine hospital in such a relatively small community. The hospital had always been important to the local people, and they made supporting it and helping it to grow over the years a priority for the entire region. The trees were bigger, and their colors spoke of autumn, but it was like a post card in my mind, perfect and unchanged.

It was like a piece of the Garden of Eden, and it was hard to believe that war had ever touched this place. But war had been a constant companion to these mountains for as long as there had been history. My grandfather had served in the First World War, and my father had served in the Second World War. Perhaps, as I sat here reflecting on my memories, that is the reason the hospital had been so important to the town.

My grandfather and my father were both tailors, and worked together in their small shop in the town. It had been many years since my Grandfather had passed away, and a great many years since my father had carried on alone in their small business. I too was a tailor, but chose to strike out on my own, seeking a place that offered me better opportunities. I have done well, and many people would recognize my name. I had traded the precious time that I might have spent with my family in Lake Braies for my fame and fortune.

The small tailor shop was now a bakery, and as I sat there this morning enjoying a cup of coffee and a pastry, I remembered what it used to look like. The large cutting tables that I had played under as a child were gone, replaced by sparkling glass cases of baked goods of every variety. The great stone fireplace was still there, and it had a nice fire in it, taking the chill off of the shop. I remember sitting under the tables while my grandfather and father worked. I would gather up the small bits and pieces of cloth that they would discard, as they worked to create a new piece of clothing. I would lay out my little treasures on the floor, trying to piece the fabric together into a creation of my own. I liked to pick up the small pieces of thread, and pretend that I was sewing the pieces together.

I spent many happy hours here, while they worked and I played and dreamed. My Grandfather liked to tell stories about the people and places he knew so well. Many times I would close my eyes and listen to his tales of the past. My favorites were his tales of what he called the Heroes of Italy, the special soldiers from our mountains. They were called "Alpini" because they grew up here in the Alps. The men from Lake Braies knew every foot of these mountains that were so critical to every war ever fought in this region. They were specially trained to fight in the mountains, and wore very distinctive hats, like a hat that Robin Hood would have worn with a feather in it.

My favorite story was about two men from our little town. They both fought in that First World War, and their story was one of friendship, and loyalty, and devotion. One was the son of a nobleman, the other a seller of flowers. They both answered the call of duty, and their friendship was forged and strengthened in the fires of battle.

There is a 15th Century castle, not far from town, on the other side of the lake. It has a very large estate with wonderful gardens and farms, and a small manmade lake. It was as beautiful as any castle in Europe. It belonged to Count Francesco Donat, and his wife Hermenia. They had a son named Giuseppe, but everyone called him Beppe. Beppe had married his college sweetheart, Lucia, and the two were just beginning their life together, awaiting the birth of their first child. They lived in the Castle with the Count and the Countess, making their happiness complete.

Many of the people from the town worked on the Estate, raising crops and livestock, and tending the gardens. The Count and his wife were kind and generous people, and respected and loved by all who knew them. Times of peace and contentment don't seem to last very long in this troubled area of the world. The clouds of war were already gathering on the horizon in 1918, pre-paring to change the lives of the people in this small town forever.

The men of the region were already enlisting in the military, and the ranks of the Alpini were swelling with the young men of Lake Braies. There was only one tavern in the town, and a large group of the Alpini was gathered there. They were enjoying the local wine, and each other's company, one last time before they would board the train and leave their homes to take up arms.

Count Francesco was very proud that his son, Beppe, would be among the volunteers of Lake Braies who would wear the green uniform and feathered hat of the Alpini. Another young man, the only florist in town, would be joining Beppe when the troop train pulled out. His name was Guido Marron, and he was a very handsome young man, always laughing and whistling a happy tune. He lived in the small apartment above his shop. He was a great favorite of the young women in Lake Braies, and never wanted for company.

As I sat there in the old train station, hearing the whistle blast from an approaching train, I remembered my grandfather's stories. I could almost see the Alpini preparing to board the train that would take them to meet their destiny. I would like to share his story with you now, in an effort to preserve a part of my childhood.

It was almost eleven o'clock in the evening on a foggy night, as a group of Alpini headed to the depot.

They were swaying from the wine of the tavern, and singing the songs of their mountains. From somewhere in the fog you could hear the approach of a car. There was only one car in the town, that of Count Francesco Donat. He and his family were taking Beppe to the train. It was a time of joy and pride, but also sadness and fear as well. Lucia was tearful as she said good bye to her husband, and Beppe promised that he would return to her, safe and sound.

On a bench, hidden by the fog, another tearful farewell was taking place. The sound of a young woman sobbing, and the reassuring voice of Guido Marron, assuring her that he too would return to her. The sound of the approaching steam locomotive interrupted their last words, as it hissed to a stop, like some great belching dragon.

The Lake Braies Alpini boarded the train, staying together for their ride to hell. As soon as they could locate an empty seat, most of the soldiers went to sleep.

Sleep didn't come easily for Guido, since he had not spent the night in the tavern with his friends. He paced restlessly up and down the narrow aisles of the train, and whistled softly to keep himself company. He eventually came to a cabin, occupied by a lone Sergeant, who was facing the window and staring out into the blackness of the night. Deciding he might as well find a place to sit, Guido knocked on the door frame and called out, "Hey, Alpino, are you alone?"

The Sergeant turned to look at him, and Guido was surprised to see his friend from elementary school. "Hey Beppe, what are you doing here? Your family is nobility; and you are their only child. You could have stayed at home, and sat this one out!"

Beppe smiled, delighted to see his old class mate. "How are you my friend? I know it probably isn't the smartest idea for me to be here, especially with Lucia expecting our first child. So many members of my family have served in the military for countless generations. It gives my father great pride to know that I am carrying on the tradition of the Donats, to serve our homeland in these troubled times."

"You were crazy when we were kids, and you are still crazy! Don't worry about it! You stick with me, and we will see this thing through together. We will give the Austrians what they have coming to them, then we will come back home to enjoy a hero's welcome."

"I feel better already just knowing you are here. If the Austrians knew that we were together, they would run screaming into the night and surrender while they still had the chance," laughed Beppe. They both laughed, and settled in for a long night of conversation and memories.

The troop train carrying the Alpini, Signeri and infantry men traveled on for many hours, bringing replacements for the front lines. When it finally arrived at its destination, the sight that greeted the soldiers as they disembarked from the train was a sobering one. The sidewalks of the station were lined with hundreds of wounded soldiers waiting for another train to transport them to the hospital.

As Guido and Beppe took in the heartbreaking vision in front of them, they looked at each other with great sadness in their eyes. Each was probably thinking that that might well be them lying on the stretchers before this was over. The Alpini who had enjoyed their last night at home drinking and singing, were now silent, shocked by the grim reality of what they would soon be facing.

Beppe was one of the few from Lake Braies that had a college education, so he would automatically start out with the rank of Sergeant. Beppe was the first to speak, knowing that he needed to help the others from Lake Braies get past this terrible sight. "Hey, all of you stay close to me. Our Captain will probably be here soon with orders for us. I will convince him that we should be kept together, since we grew up together, and we work well together as a team."

Guido, understanding Beppe's intention to try and pull the men together, and get them to focus on something more positive called out, "Hey, Alpini, don't you sing anymore? Did you break your voices with too much wine last night in the tavern? Let's sing something for these brave men, so they will know who we are!"

With that, the men began to sing, softly at first, but picking up more volume and spirit as their ranks swelled. They sang of home and their mountains, and the honor of defending their families and country. As they sang, a

Captain approached them, as they were standing on the platform. He was a short man with graying hair, and from the empty sleeve on his uniform, it was clear that he was no stranger to the war.

The Captain listened for a moment, then spoke up, "Very good Alpini, I am glad you are in good spirits tonight. Which one of you is Sergeant Donat?"

"I am here, Captain," spoke up Beppe, raising his hand.

"Very well, Sergeant. Form your Alpini on the street. There is a troop transport, with mules, that will take you to your assigned position on top of that hill. Deploy your men in the trenches on the side of the hill, and wait for further orders from headquarters. Oh, and Sergeant, are you related to Count Francesco Donat?

"Yes Sir, he is my father." Beppe spoke up with pride.

"You might be interested to know that your father and my father served in the Calvary together in the last war. Good luck to you and your men, Sergeant!"

"Thank you, Sir, that is good to know. Good luck to you too." Beppe smiled in return as the Captain turned to leave.

After they arrived at their post, and fanned out through the trenches ringing the hill top, the Alpini shared the last of the Grappa, the wine from their vineyards of Lake Braies. Sergeant Donat, and his new second in command, Corporal Marron, stayed close to each other. They vowed to look after each other and their friends, and they worked hard to keep that promise.

During the long night in the trenches, Sergeant Donat had time to write to his family out of the small notebook he kept in his shirt pocket.

He let them know they had arrived safely, and all of the Alpini from Lake Braies were together. He spoke of his love for them, and his hope that they would be able to end this war quickly. He didn't mention the things he had seen, or the deafening roar of the cannons as they fired round after round through the night. The Alpini were quiet, and Beppe broke the silence to help them think about something else besides the sound of the enemy's machine-gun fire. "Hey, Guido, is there someone back at home for you to write to?"

"No," came the one word response from Guido, perhaps a little too quickly.

"I can't believe a handsome man like you doesn't have someone in Lake Braies to worry about them," Beppe teased Guido.

"No," came the answer again, but this time there was a noticeable hesitation in Guido's voice. "Well, there is one girl . . ." Guido paused as if he was thinking about her. "She is a very nice girl."

"Oh, I see! Don't keep me in suspense, tell me about her!" Beppe said, with real interest in his expression.

"Her name is Maria," Guido's voice faded again, as if he were remembering something important. "She is a very nice girl."

Beppe laughed, "You already said that, tell me about her!"

Guido smiled to hide his embarrassment. "Sergeant, are you prying into my private life?"

"Of course I am! We haven't seen each other for a very long time, and I am just trying to get caught up on your life, so give!" Beppe waited, with his arms crossed, not letting Guido off the hook.

"I have only been out with her a few times, and I like her very much. She isn't like anyone else I have ever met. She is a simple girl, and she is so easy to talk to, like I have known her all of my life. She listens to me, and seems to know what I am feeling. When we left Lake Braies last night, she saw me off at the train depot. She was very sad that I was leaving, and she gave me a kiss and a hug good bye. She is an orphan, and it made her nervous that something bad might happen to someone else in her life. She was raised by Nuns in a convent. She is a maid for one of the wealthiest families in town, and they think very highly of her, like one of their own family. Poor Maria, it broke my heart to see the tears in her eyes as the train pulled out of the station. She hasn't had it very easy in her life, and I could see how hard it was for her to watch me leave."

"So," responded Beppe, "That was her I heard in the fog on the bench at the station crying and saying good-bye."

"I would think that is true, there weren't many people near us at the time," Guido replied, thinking of their farewell.

At that moment, Captain Alfresi arrived, breaking up the melancholy moment, as they thought about the ones they left behind. He was the officer who had met them at the train, and given them their marching orders. He was hard to mistake for another Captain, with his missing left arm. He was probably here to bring them the orders they had been waiting for from their headquarters.

"Sergeant Donat," the Captain called in the darkness.

"Yes, Sir," answered Beppe, ready to receive his orders.

"You and your Alpini will be issued a radio, field telephone, shovels, machine-guns and ammunition. Just before sunrise, head for the top of the mountain, and position yourselves so you can see the valley below. We will need reports of any enemy troop movements, and any formations you spot. This information is vital to our mission, and we are counting on you to be our eyes and ears." The Captain handed Beppe a written set of his orders, and headed off into the darkness.

"Yes, Sir," Beppe called after him. He gave the signal for the men to get ready to move out.

They were at their positions at the top of the mountain for over two weeks, dug in and watching any movements below them. They regularly sent word to units farther down the mountain, to be relayed back to headquarters. The Austrians, when they finally spotted the Alpini, gave them a warm greeting with their machine guns and grenades. They returned their welcome to the neighborhood with a withering round of fire of their own. They encouraged the Austrians to keep their heads down and be content to stay in their trenches. Their mission would have been a complete success, but sadly they lost one of the Alpini. He threw himself on a grenade lobbed into the trench, saving his friends. He was killed instantly. It would be the first of many sad letters to families in Lake Braies.

Captain Fressi, from headquarters, was very pleased with the success of the mission, and granted a day of rest at the rear of the lines. They had hot food to eat, and beds to sleep in for a change, and their mail finally caught up with them. Beppe was delighted to get a letter from his wife, Lucia. He didn't take long to find a quiet place to read a letter that was more important to him than anything else.

"My Dearest Beppe, I miss you so much, and the days are so long without you. I treasure our last night together, and look forward to the day when you will come home to us again. Since you have gone, we are receiving more reports of the war from the front.

Your father is constantly reading everything he can get his hands on, and talking to anyone who has had news of the battles. He is so proud of you and the other Alpini from Lake Braies, but he worries about you too. He knows that our family has a long history of military service, but you are his only child and he can't help but worry that your strong sense of duty could result in you being hurt or killed.

We stay busy with the work of the Estate, growing extra food for the war effort. We are so glad that you have your friend Guido with you. We try to comfort each other and we pray for you and all of our soldiers. We pray you will all return to us. Love from me and your mother and your father. Be safe my love."

Chapter Two

In the weary months that followed, the war that seemed like it would be short dragged on, extracting a heavy toll in injuries and death. The cold weather had set in and the rain and the snow were their constant companions in this trying and unhappy ordeal.

The group of Alpini was holding up to the rigors of war, and they were gaining a reputation for getting difficult missions accomplished. Captain Fressi was a frequent visitor, and he arrived with new orders for them.

"Alpini" the Captain began, with hesitation in his voice, "headquarters is asking you for another delicate mission. This mission is different from anything we have asked from you before, and extremely dangerous. That is why we are only asking for volunteers this time. You will have two hours to decide, and no one will think any less of you if you don't accept the mission. Keep in mind this is a request, not an order, it is strictly up to you."

The band of Alpini, friends and brothers all, looked at each other, and nodded their intent. "Captain Fressi" Beppe interrupted him, before he could turn to go, "We will accept whatever assignment you have for us." The men, veterans of dozens of difficult missions, looked back at their Captain, waiting for his orders.

Captain Fressi was openly touched by the unwavering support given to him by his men. There was no hesitation or question in their minds, even when he gave them an opportunity to decline this mission. There was a lump of pride and gratitude in his chest, and he had to clear his throat before he could speak.

"Thank you my Alpini, I am very proud of all of you. We have a large number of cannons and munitions waiting for you. You will spearhead a mission to stop the advance of enemy troops toward our lines. Our division will be supported by divisions from both the French and the British armies. They are not close enough to our position at present, and you will have to hold our lines by yourselves until they can arrive. Thank you for accepting the mission to assure our hold on this mountain so critical to our success. God bless and keep you all."

They immediately deployed to their positions, and positioned the gun emplacements not realizing that they would be holding this precious piece of high ground for four long months. Their position was of vital strategic importance, as it commanded a view of the entire valley below them.

The enemy wasn't long in pressing their claim to the position. They had a 420mm cannon they named the Barbarian. The Italian guns were not as big, but their hearts, their skill, and their determination equalized the fight. The Austrians were finally reinforced by the

German 2nd Battalion of the Alpine Corp. Hopelessly outgunned and outnumbered; the orders for the Italian retreat finally reached the Alpini from headquarters.

There were hundreds and hundreds of soldiers on both sides killed and thousands more injured on that bloody battle of wills for the ownership of Mt. San Michelle. One of the Alpini was injured but refused to be evacuated. Pasqual Dell'Orco was a carpenter by trade. Injured and unable to fight, he made caskets for his comrades that fell in the fighting. Forty years later his bravery and sacrifice was rewarded when it came to light, by the Italian Government, with the Citation of Cavaliere. It was a source of pride for the whole town, especially his son, Tony.

Even though the Italian Army was forced to retreat from their mountaintop, the mission was a complete success. They had stopped the advance of the enemy troops, and delayed them long enough to bring another vital part of their plan into play. They were able to construct a special pontoon bridge across the Piave River, allowing the Italian Army to attack their enemy from the rear. It was a devastating blow to the Austrian and German forces, but it was paid for by the blood of those loyal Alpini troops. Even today the mountain is dotted with crosses, paying silent tribute to those unknown men.

Beppe and Guido were able to stay together, in spite of all of the chaos and cannon fire surrounding them. During that final night they found shelter in a trench filled with snow and debris, waiting out the fight until first light. The order to retreat came soon after sunrise, and they were preparing to move out.

The sound of another incoming round caught Guido's attention, and he spun around to locate the direction of the shell. He screamed to Beppe, warning him to take cover, knocking his friend to the ground. The shells and grenades and machine-gun fire were raining down on their position, as the enemy tried to cut off their retreat. Guido came to, some time later, dazed and struggling to get his bearings. He was still on top of Beppe, where he had knocked his friend to the ground in a desperate bid to save him.

Beppe had a bad head wound, but he was still alive; Guido's body had protected him from the brunt of the blast.

Guido reached over and tried to wake Beppe up. "Beppe, open your eyes. We promised that we would take care of each other. You can't make a liar out of me and leave me now!" Guido was so intent on his friend, that he didn't realize that he was wounded too. He had been hit by the same shell, and his left leg was bleeding badly. He had caught a part of the shell casing that had injured Beppe. There was no one alive in their area, so Guido painfully moved on his damaged leg and searched through the packs of the dead Alpini. He found some liquor in one pack, and used it to disinfect his leg wound, and Beppe's head wound.

Guido stared down the mountain, trying to decide how he was going to get Beppe to safety. He wouldn't be able to carry him because of his leg. He rounded up some ropes and belts, and attached them to some broken tree branches. He rolled Beppe onto the makeshift sled, and tied it around his shoulders. He struggled for hours, dragging his dear friend behind. He couldn't say how long he had toiled to get him down the mountain. He just kept putting one foot in front of the other, never giving up; hope would be the last thing to die.

Guido spotted a fresh field of snow, and with the grim determination of a man who had nothing left to lose, he tied the ropes and belts around Beppe and himself more tightly. Before committing himself to the steep slope, he raised his eyes to heaven and called out, "God, we are in your hands now, please help us." With that, he pushed off with all of the strength he had left, and hung on for dear life.

By some miracle the cobbled together sled held together, and they made it to the bottom of the slope in one piece. Still bleeding and in pain, Guido slowly limped over to check on Beppe. He was unconscious, but still breathing. With that, Guido passed out, too weak to fight for their lives any longer.

Guido awoke two days later in a hospital near Trento. The first thing he saw was the face of a Nun tending to his wounds, and wiping the sweat off of his face.

"How are you, my son?" asked the Nun, with a look of concern on her face.

"Where am I?" asked Guido, looking around him, unable to get his bearings.

"You are in Trento, in the hospital," the Sister replied, with an encouraging smile.

"And the Sergeant that was near me, Sergeant Donat, where is he?!" Guido asked, looking around him, with mounting panic in his voice.

"Calm yourself, thanks to you he will be all right soon. You saved his life bringing him down the mountain, it was a miracle." She wiped his face again, and rang a bell to call the doctor. He arrived a few minutes later and smiled at Guido, as he walked around the privacy curtain.

"Good morning to you Hero, it is good to see you awake. How are you feeling?" the doctor asked with a grin on his face.

"Why am I a Hero?" asked Guido, with a confused look.

"You are a Hero because you saved your Sergeant's life. He is still in a coma, but I believe he will live and make a full recovery, thanks to you. The story is all over the hospital of how you got him down the mountain. The soldiers who found the two of you couldn't believe how far you dragged him. They said it must have taken you hours, and with your own serious injuries. Unbelievable." The doctor checked Guido's chart, and looked as if he had something else on his mind. "I am afraid the rest of the news is not so good." The doctor glanced at the Nun, trying to go on.

"You couldn't save my leg, could you? I knew it was bad, but I didn't have any other option, I had to help my friend." Guido looked at the doctor, as if he were trying to apologize for injuring his own leg on purpose.

"Yes, I had to remove part of your leg. Gangrene had already set in by the time they got you to the hospital, and you would have been dead in a few hours if I didn't remove the infected part. I am sorry." The doctor looked closely at Guido, waiting for his reaction.

"Doctor, it could have been worse I suppose, I still have my other leg. I left a lot of my friends up on that mountain. They weren't as lucky as me, I am still alive. It will be different, to be sure, but I will figure it out and get along just fine." Guido smiled up at the doctor and the Sister.

The sacrifice of the Alpini soldiers on that terrible mountain turned the tide of the war. They delayed the enemy long enough for British Forces and French Forces to reinforce the Italian Forces. Facing far less favorable odds, and with the approach of another brutal winter, the Austrian and German Governments had no choice but to sue for peace.

The War was finally over, and Captain Fressi made his way to the hospital to visit the few survivors of the men entrusted to his care of that costly engagement. One of his first stops was to see Corporal Guido Marron.

Captain Fressi stuck his head around the corner of the door and saw Guido sitting there in bed. As soon as Guido noticed who it was, he struggled to get to the edge of the bed and try to stand up, showing the Captain proper military courtesy.

"At ease, Sergeant, at ease! You need to rest. How are you doing, my hero? The Captain said, gently putting his hand on Guido's shoulder, and pushing him back down onto the bed.

"I am fine, Sir. I have been better, but at least I am still alive. I think so many of the truly heroic Alpini were not as fortunate." Guido looked back at the Captain, with a sincere face that said he believed what he had just said.

"Sergeant Guido Marron, it is my great pleasure to inform you of your promotion, and to present you with this medal, our highest award, from a grateful nation. Your heroic efforts to rescue Captain Donat, under impossible odds with great risk to yourself, is a credit to you and every man who has ever shared this uniform with you! Is there anything I can do for you? Is there anything that you need?" The Captain stared down at Guido, in awe of this humble man.

Those who had cared for Guido at the hospital were very touched, not only by his promotion and his medal, but by the man himself. This simple man who genuinely believed his actions were nothing out of the ordinary. He was just doing his duty as a soldier, and keeping his word as a friend. He didn't understand what all of the fuss was about, but the doctor and the Nuns did.

"It has been an honor to know you and Captain Donat. I repeat: is there anything that I can do for you before I have to leave?" The Captain asked.

"I would very much like to be moved to the room where Captain Donat is recovering. I would like to be there when he wakes up. This may be hard for him to understand, and it would be easier if a friend is there for him." Guido looked at the Captain earnestly, as if he were asking for a very large favor.

"That's not up to me, son, I think that is something the doctor would have to approve. Will that be a problem, Doctor?" The captain looked at the doctor.

"Of course not, we will be happy to move the sergeant to the captain's room right away. It would definitely be good for both of them to be together and help each other's recoveries." The doctor nodded to the Sister, to let her know that she could move him right away.

"Good luck to you, Sergeant. We both know what it is to sacrifice for our country. Never be ashamed of your injury; you can go on with your life and do whatever you choose. I have." With that, the two wounded soldiers shook hands, and the captain went on his way to do what he could for others in the hospital.

While Guido and Beppe were in the hospital, Italy began the slow and painful task of rebuilding from the long and brutal war. She was not alone in this daunting task, with aid coming from the United States, England and France.

In the Castle of Count Donat, another small miracle came to help ease the terrible losses of Lake Braies. Lucia gave birth to a beautiful blonde baby boy named Paul. He was named after his great grandfather Paul Donat, Cavalier to King Umberto of Italy. Lucia wanted nothing more than to be with Beppe in the hospital, but the birth of their new son, and the fragile health of both of Beppe's parents, won't permit it. The Count's weak heart was failing, and he was in very grave condition. Donna Hermenia's health was also failing because of all of the stress and worry she has endured. Lucia must stay home and take care of them, but her heart longed to be with her husband as well.

Everyone in the region heard the news of Beppe and Guido's heroic actions on the mountain, as well as their miraculous survival. It was a proud and happy moment for Lake Braies in the middle of so much grief and despair for the loss of the other Alpini. It gave them hope that they will be able to rebuild their own lives, and go forward after the terrible tragedy.

Lucia wrote to Beppe, knowing he will eventually emerge from his coma. She wanted to give him hope, and a reason to live, by knowing he is the father of a beautiful healthy baby. She wrote of her love and her longing to hold him again, keeping the letter positive and up-beat. She did not mention the failing health of his parents, knowing there is nothing he can do, and the worry would not help his own recovery. She added his mother has been afforded the title of "Donna," to pay respect to her a member of this noble family and her valiant heart.

In Trento, Beppe was still in a coma, but he gradually showed signs that he is becoming aware of things around him. Guido was always by his side, talking to him, reading to him, and whistling his cheerful tunes. Somewhere in his dreamless fog, Beppe began to hear the familiar whistling of his childhood friend, and tried to respond and follow the sound.

"This is a very good sign," comments the doctor. "Guido, you should talk to him, talk about anything. Let him hear your voice, he is trying to find his way back to us. Keep doing what ever you have been doing, it is working."

Two days later, Captain Beppe Donat opened his eyes for the first time since he was hit on the mountain. The first thing he saw was the face of his faithful friend Guido, grinning at him like a cat with feathers in his mouth.

"Guido! Where am I? Where are we? How did we get here? Where are our men?" Beppe looked around the room, confused and panicked.

"Hey Captain! It is about time you woke up! You have been lying around this room too long getting fat and lazy. We are in a hospital in Trento, and the War is over. We beat those Russka sewer rats, and sent them hightailing it for home. When you are recovered, we will go home to Lake Braies." Guido grinned, relieved to see his friends eyes open, and to hear his voice again after so long.

"What about you, why are you in bed? Are you all right? What happened, I don't remember anything after you yelled my name." Beppe said in a worried voice, looking over at Guido.

"I'm OK. The incoming round exploded, hitting my leg, and they had to take part of my leg off. Let's call the doctor and the Nuns, they sure will be happy to see that you are finally awake!" Guido reached over and rang the bell by his bed. The doctor and the Sister were there in a flash, knowing Beppe was close to awakening.

"Well, there is our other hero! How are you feeling?" the doctor smiled with relief.

"I feel dizzy and confused, why did you call me a hero?" asked Beppe, blinking like an owl in sunlight.

"That is normal, after what you have been through" answered the doctor, making some notes on his chart. "I called you a hero, Captain, because you are a hero, both you and Sergeant Marron. The action of the Alpini on that mountain was responsible in part for us winning the war. The sergeant is a double hero because he saved your life, getting you down after you were hurt," the doctor explained.

"Guido, I am still confused. Why are they calling me Captain, and you Sergeant? You saved my life, and I don't remember a thing, talk to me!" Beppe appealed to Guido.

"I promised that I would look out for you, before we left home. It was my duty to see that you came home safe and sound. Captain Fressi was here a while ago, to give us both promotions for our actions on holding our positions on Mt. San Michelle. I am afraid not too many of us made it back alive. We will receive pensions for our injuries. We will be going home pretty soon, you are a new father, and you have responsibilities to see to! What do you think, my friend?" Guido laughed with glee to see the understanding and the joy in his friend's face.

A few days later, Captain Donat was given permission to go home and finish recovering there, if he wanted to.

"What about Guido?" Beppe asked, in a somber voice.

"The sergeant isn't ready to be discharged yet. We have more exams to do on his leg; he still has shrapnel so there is the risk of more infection. It might be necessary to remove more of his leg if there are complications with his healing. Once he is out of the woods, he still has to go through therapy to learn how to get around on his crutches safely," answered the doctor, being honest about Guido's recovery.

"In that case, I will stay here and recover with him. We came together, and we will return home the same way, together." Beppe replied, intent on supporting his friend.

The great day finally arrived for Guido and Beppe to return home. It was hard saying good bye to all of the hospital staff who had been there for them, especially the Doctor, and Sister Angelina. They were such an inspiration to everyone in the hospital. Guido never lost his sense of humor and was always a real moral booster to other soldiers that were undergoing rehabilitation. They would be sorely missed.

Captain Donat was always there for Sergeant Marron, through all of his painful recovery. He couldn't shake the feeling of guilt when he watched his friend struggling to learn to use his crutches. He prayed for him often, that he would find a place in the world, with such an uncertain future.

"Sister Angelina, smile for me, you look so sad. This is a happy day; I will be going home to a Hero's welcome, and everyone in Lake Braies will be there to greet me," Guido encouraged the tearful Nun.

Reaching into her pocket, she pulled out a cross and handed it to him. "This cross was given to my mother when I entered the Order. I want you to have it now. It will help you to remember us, and remember that God loves you and that we are praying for your future."

As Guido put the cross around his neck he asked the Sister, "May I ask you a personal question?"

"Of course, what would you like to know?" Angelina replied.

"Despite your age, you still have lovely eyes. I am sure you must have been a beautiful woman when you were younger. I have had the most wonderful Angel tending to me while I have been recovering. Will you have a cup of tea with me before I leave?" Guido smiled in appreciation.

"I would enjoy having a cup of tea with you. That is the nicest offer I have had in a long time." The Sister smiled.

Guido's eyes grew large, as he tasted his first sip of tea. "Wow! That is more Grappa than tea. Where did you get it?"

"My brother brings me some when he comes to visit me. I thank you for your kind words, but what we look like doesn't have anything to do with our decisions to enter the Lord's service. We do it because we wish to serve God by caring for His children. I have watched over you since the day you came to us, and I have noticed that you don't seem to be a particularly religious man. Would you mind telling me why?" Angelina asked, looking at Guido with concern.

"I don't know, Sister," Guido said thoughtfully, "My mother died when I was very young, and my father did the best he could to raise me. He wasn't a very religious man either, but after my mother died he seemed to be very bitter. He devoted himself to me and to his flowers. I think he felt that God forgot about him."

To brighten the conversation Angelina said "You are a very handsome man yourself, Sergeant. There must be some young woman waiting at home for you."

"Perhaps, I am not certain. There was a woman I was just starting to get to know when I left for war. She was a wonderful person, gentle and caring, and I enjoyed being with her. I don't know if she would want to be with someone like me, in my condition. I never heard anything from her since I left Lake Braies; perhaps she found someone else." Guido had a far away look in his eyes, remembering the girl he had left behind.

Beppe showed up to get Guido, having made all of their travel arrangements. Guido kissed Sister Angelina's work worn hands and thanked her for her help and prayers. They took a cab to the train station, with what little luggage they had with them. The train was waiting for them, to escort the two heroes of Lake Braies home. There was a special nurse waiting on the platform to care for Guido on the trip home, and a great many people from Trento to send them off. The cabin they rode home in was a great deal more comfortable than the one that had taken them to the front. The Railroad spared no expense to see that they were comfortable and well taken care of.

"Hey," crowed Guido, "This is pretty nice! It is so good to finally be on our way home." Beppe just smiled at his friend, and nodded in agreement.

Chapter Three

As the train cleared the last tunnel before arriving at the Depot in Lake Braies, they could hear the strains of the local band. The music was very loud, and it attracted Guido's and Beppe's attention. They looked out the window to see where the music was coming from. From their seats they could see that the station was jam packed with people, and there were Italian flags and welcome home banners everywhere. The whole town had turned out to welcome their two heroes home.

As the train came to a stop, Beppe helped Guido get to his feet, and adjusted his crutches. "I wonder who is on the train with us, General Cadorna?" asked Guido, as he ducked his head to peek out of the windows.

"No you numbskull, they are here to welcome us home! We are some of the few Alpini who have made it back, so we have to be cheerful and happy. We are the sons they will never be able to welcome home again. Smile, we are finally home!" Beppe encouraged his amazed friend.

Two male nurses came aboard to help Guido get down off of the train safely. A man on crutches isn't too graceful getting up and down train steps. Beppe waved them off, and helped Guido set foot on the soil of home himself.

Lucia Donat and her son Paul were waiting on the platform for Beppe, but there were so many people pressing forward to greet both men it was hard to make any headway in the crowd. Beppe finally spotted his wife and son, and made a grab for them, hugging his wife as if he would never let her go. He picked up his son for the first time, and stared at him, memorizing every feature of his face. Then he remembered Guido, and pulled him away from all of his well wishers to meet his family. Guido was still scanning the crush of people for the one person he was hoping to see.

"Lucia, this is my dear friend Guido Marron. We have been together every day since the train pulled out taking us to the front. I wouldn't be here if it weren't for Guido; he saved my life and brought me safely home. He was the Florist here in town, and he will be staying with us until he is better able to manage on his own." Beppe grinned at Guido, with his arm around his shoulder.

Lucia grabbed Guido and hugged him and kissed his cheeks, with tears of gratitude running down her face. "Thank you. You will always be welcome in our home!" she affirmed with a grateful smile. No other words are necessary between people who share such a bond of friendship and devotion.

Guido was grateful for her kind words, but he was still distracted, scanning the crowd for the face he longed to see more than anything else. He had no luck catching sight of her.

Among the people who were also absent from the welcome at the station was Beppe's father. He had passed away several months ago, and Lucia thought it was better to keep the news from him, so he wouldn't have a setback in his recovery. She felt he would be better able to deal with his father's death when he arrived back home, surrounded by friends and family to help him deal with his loss.

His mother was waiting for him at home. She had a very difficult time since his departure, and her health since her dear husband's passing had been very fragile. Hermenia was sitting on a comfortable sofa, wearing her mourning clothes, waiting impatiently for Beppe's arrival. She knew he was coming home, but it has been so long and the war has been so terrible, she could hardly make herself believe that he was really coming home.

Beppe rushed into the room and took his mother in his arms. They were both crying, with great joy and the sadness of Francesco's passing. Beppe heard the sound of Guido's crutches on the floor behind him, and finally let his mother go.

"This is my dear friend Guido. He used to be the florist here in town. He will be staying with us for a while." Beppe held out his hand to Guido, beckoning him to come and greet his mother.

Donna Hermenia was well acquainted with her son's best friend, through all of the letters Beppe has written since he has been gone. "Of course I know Guido; you always came with your father when he delivered flowers to us. I will never be able to thank you enough for what you have done for us by bringing Beppe home. This is your home now. I hope you will be able to bring me more beautiful flowers that you have grown yourself very soon. We can all use a little beauty in our lives, especially now." She hugged Guido, and anyone looking at them would have thought that they were indeed family.

"I will do my very best to see that you have flowers as lovely as you are, dear lady." Guido hugged her very gently, grateful for his warm welcome.

Chapter Four

Beppe settled Guido into a nice little single story cottage on the Castle grounds, not far from his quarters. It was surrounded by pine trees and beautiful flowers. He had a personal assistant to help him with all of his daily needs. The two friends were constantly together, eating, talking, walking, or working. You never saw one man without the other close by.

As Guido regained his strength, he turned his attention to the gardens of the Estate. During the war they were neglected because the crops and the livestock were more important. There just weren't enough people to see to everything. Guido devoted long hours bringing the gardens back to life. It was good for his soul to see the beautiful flowers and bushes responding to his expert care. He loved bringing armfuls of flowers up to the Castle for Donna Hermenia, in a special bag that he could carry over his shoulder.

The months pass, and the men healed from their wounds, both physically and emotionally. Every Saturday Beppe made the trip to the market fair in the carriage. He bought supplies, and dropped off produce from the Estate to the merchants. One time he talked Guido into going with him and they visited the only tavern in the town.

Guido was well known at the tavern, and there were other Alpini back from the war. They drank the wine, and shared their tales, and sang the songs of their mountains that helped them remember happier times. There were a lot of nice young women at the tavern, to sing and celebrate the return of the men from Lake Braies. Beppe could see that Guido was happy and content as they drove back to the Castle in the carriage. It had been too long since Guido had enjoyed the companionship of a nice woman, and he was happy that his friend's missing leg did not stop him from feeling like a whole man again.

Beppe looked at Guido. He was content, but was he really happy? He didn't think so. He put on a brave face, but there was something missing. They were both feeling the effects of all the wine they enjoyed and they were still singing the songs they were singing in the tavern. Guido was a little drunk and rested his head on his friend's shoulder.

"Guido, do you remember the nice girl you told me about, the one who saw you off at the train station the night we left? She was crying in the fog and was so sad to see you leave." Beppe ventured, trying to get Guido to talk about this mysterious woman.

"Of course I remember her, her name was Maria. She used to come into my shop often to buy flowers for her employer, Dr. Marron. She worked for the family many years as a maid, and they loved her like part of their family." Guido said, the wine helped him talk about the woman he never mentioned.

Beppe slowed the pace of the horses, so he could better listen to Guido. He was anxious to find out something about this woman Guido thought so highly of. "What ever happened to her? She wasn't at the station when we came home?"

"I don't know, she just disappeared," Guido spoke from the darkness.

"That's crazy, people don't just disappear!" Beppe pressed for more information.

"I asked around about her, after we got back. They said she quit her job and left the city shortly after we left for the war," Guido added, remembering his disappointment.

"Where do you think she might have gone?" Beppe asked, hoping to keep Guido on the subject.

"She was an orphan, raised in the Convent of Carmelitane, by the Sisters there. She wanted to be a nun at one time in her life, but changed her mind and left the Convent. She felt she didn't have what it took to be a good nun." With that Guido drifted off to sleep.

When they arrived home, Beppe helped him into bed. Guido was too drunk to even get undressed, so he covered up his friend and bid him good night.

The next morning, Beppe was sitting in the garden reading the newspaper when he heard the familiar sound of his friend's crutches approaching on the stone walk.

"Are you finally awake? I thought perhaps you had too much fun last night and decided to sleep the whole day away!" grinned Beppe.

"I have a killer headache; I can't believe we drank so much wine last night. We must have drained the tavern dry." Guido held his head in his hands.

"Have some of that strong coffee there on the table, you will feel better in no time," laughed Beppe. "I went to early Mass in the town this morning."

"Why, you have your own chapel here in the Castle," commented Guido, drinking his second cup of coffee. "What did you need to go to Mass in Lake Braies for?"

"I was hoping to run into Dr Marron at church, and inquire after Maria. Perhaps he knows where she is working." Guido looked up, waiting for Beppe to go on.

"I didn't see the Doctor, but I ran into his sister outside of the church, and asked about Maria." Beppe knew he had Guido's full attention by the way he was staring at him, waiting for him to continue.

"She said that Maria left their service right after we left for war, without giving them any notice. She thought that was very strange, since Maria had worked for them for so long, and was just like a member of their family," ended Beppe waiting for his friend to say something.

"That is very odd, she wasn't like that at all" was all Guido said, but he was obviously thinking about this new bit of information.

Spring finally arrived, with a rush of flowers and the promise of warm sunshine. Guido's efforts in the gardens began to show real progress. They were almost back to their former glory, before the dark times of the war. Lucia was a frequent visitor to the gardens, gathering bouquets to brighten up the Castle sitting rooms. Guido was always nervous that his flowers weren't good enough for the Castle, but he was really very proud of all that he had been able to accomplish.

The hills started to sport their new coat of green, as the snow grudgingly gave up its claim to the mountain. Paul was growing faster than the gardens, and was becoming a very handsome boy. He loved his Uncle Guido, and followed him everywhere. Paul was probably more of a hindrance to Guido than a help, but he loved the boy so much, that he didn't mind having to do some things over again. Guido quietly replanted a new set of flowers that Paul had helped him with by the big fountain, and he hoped the boy wouldn't notice the difference. It was the second Easter since the war ended, and he could feel the rebirth of the earth all around him.

The bells from all of the bell towers in the town were ringing, announcing the coming of the spring fair. The girls wore their new spring dresses, much to the appreciation of the young men in Lake Braies. The evidence of the war was still everywhere to be seen. There were buildings that hadn't been rebuilt yet, but no one seemed to talk about them any more, as the weeds slowly erased them from sight.

The mountains bore mute evidence of the many thousands of soldiers who had lost their lives in the bloody struggles for supremacy. They were covered with simple wooden crosses, marking the places where they fell. There were so many, from a distance they looked more like a field of flowers than wooden markers.

Chapter Five

On Easter Sunday morning, a letter was delivered to Guido unexpectedly from the distant city of Udine. He couldn't imagine who would be writing to him, as he knew no one in that city. He found Beppe in his office, putting some of the Estate's paperwork in order. It was a curious letter, asking if Guido was from a certain address in Lake Braies, and, if so, requesting that he come to Udine. The two friends had no idea what the letter was about, but decided to accept the invitation, and make the long trip to Udine.

Beppe and Guido set out in the car the next day, early in the morning and arrived in Udine in the afternoon. They talked on the way, speculating what the letter might mean, and were both stumped as to its origin and its intent. "I guess we will see when we get there," said Beppe, when they finally ran out of ideas.

The address took them to a very large old building with small windows and a big door. There were iron bars on the windows, and an old brass knocker on the door. They knocked, and after a moment, the window in the door opened. The woman who answered was small and almost completely covered by a white habit.

"Greetings gentlemen, how may we be of service?" the woman asked in a polite voice.

"I am Count Donat, and my companion is Mr. Guido Marron from Lake Braies. He received a letter asking us to come here; perhaps we have the wrong address." Beppe ventured, waiting to see what the woman would say.

"No, no," came the answer from the small pale face. "This is the right address; please wait there a moment while I open the door for you."

When the old door finally swung open, the two visitors from Lake Braies were standing face to face with a nun dressed in a very long black robe. "Welcome, gentlemen" intoned the small woman in a very excited voice. "I am Sister Felice; please follow me."

Guido and Beppe exchanged astonished looks, but obediently followed the black clad woman like two small boys on their first day of school. She stopped at the entrance to a small garden with a wooden bench. "Please have a seat; the mother Superior will be with you shortly. You must be tired after such a long trip. I will bring you some refreshments while you wait. You are most welcome here in the Convent." With that the tiny figure in the floor length robes was gone.

Guido and Beppe sat down on the bench without a word, and looked around them. There was a small statue of the Madonna, and the birds were singing in the trees.

There were a number of arched corridors surrounding the carefully tended garden. The corridors were lined with countless small wooden doors, all of them closed.

"What do you think?" asked Guido, finally breaking the silence.

"I have absolutely no idea, my friend" remarked Beppe, still looking around him. "I thought it was strange that the Sister seemed to be expecting us. How would she know who we are?"

At that moment Sister Felice came bustling back into view, carrying a small tray with glasses of water and biscuits. "I hope you like our biscuits; we make them here at the Convent ourselves. Everyone who tries them says they are the best they have ever tasted. Enjoy. The mother Superior has been advised of your arrival." With that the small woman turned and was gone from sight.

As they munched thoughtfully on their biscuits, they felt like Sister Felice might be the only other person here. Then slowly there was the sound of doors opening up softly all over the courtyard. As each door opened, a Nun, dressed similarly to the tiny Sister came out of her cell, and quietly took a seat on the wooden bench outside of their door. All of their eyes were on the two guests to their Convent, and there was an air of expectancy as they sat there, silently regarding the men.

Beppe and Guido couldn't shake the feeling that something important was about to happen, by the look of all of the assembled Sisters. Another door swung open farther down the corridor, and a new Nun came into view. She was much taller that Sister Felice and she walked with a certain dignity in her gait that left no doubt that this was the mother Superior. The two friends felt like they would be getting some answers to their questions very soon.

"I am Sister Benedettina, the mother Superior of this Convent, welcome, and thank you for coming." She was dressed all in white, and had a very large black sash around her robes. A long set of beads and a crucifix hung from the sash.

Beppe rose to his feet immediately, out of respect, but Guido remained seated because of his disability. After looking over both of her guests, the mother Superior, noticing Guido's crutches, said, "You must be Mr. Guido Marron."

"You are correct mother. May I introduce Count Giuseppe Donat, my good friend and loyal companion? He likes to be called Beppe." Guido was very nervous, and was trying hard not to shake.

"Please have a seat, Count Donat" the mother gestured with her hand. Sister Felice brought a chair for her, and she joined them as they sat in the beautiful garden, waiting for answers.

Guido couldn't contain his nerves any longer and spoke with a tremble in his voice. "Please mother Superior, why have you asked me here, to this beautiful place of peace?"

"We read accounts of your great heroism during the war in the newspaper. We understand that you, Mr.

Marron, even saved Count Donat's life." The mother looked at him with eyes that possessed infinite patience and wisdom.

"With all due respect, mother, I doubt that you have summoned us here to congratulate us on our war records." Guido was clearly on edge, and trying desperately not to be rude.

The mother Superior leaned closer to Guido, and smiled. "Yes of course, you are quite right. First of all, thank you for calling me mother, someone I believe we both know also called me mother. I believe you knew our Maria, who worked for a number of years for Dr. Marron in Lake Braies?"

"Yes" answered Guido in a whisper, the sweat evident on his face as he hung on her every word. "Please mother, if you have word of her, tell me! I have been searching for her ever since I returned from the hospital in Trento. I have not heard from her, it is like she has disappeared from the face of the earth!"

The nun picked up the beads from her sash, and began to run her fingers over them, considering what she wanted to say next. "My son, you seem to be a good and honorable man. I was unsure if I should attempt to contact you, but after making it a matter of fasting and prayer, I decided to ask you to come see me."

At that moment, Beppe moved closer to his friend, and put his arm around him, knowing the reason for their trip was about to be made know to them, and he felt that it was very important.

"Maria was abandoned as an infant on our front door, and was raised here at the convent. This was her home for many years. Maria had considered becoming a member of our order for a time, but decided she didn't have the devotion necessary to become a nun. Dr. Marron is my cousin, so after speaking with him, I decided to send Maria to him when she left the convent, to secure employment. She worked for the Marron family for a long time, and was very happy there. Maria returned to us some weeks after you left to go to the front lines. She was pregnant, and she didn't know where else to turn. She was ashamed, and she didn't want to burden the Marron family with a scandal, as they had been so kind to her. She didn't know if you would ever return from the fighting, so many of our brave soldiers never returned home. She stayed here with us, awaiting the birth of her child. She delivered a beautiful baby girl, and was able to hold her for a short while, before she died due to complications from the difficult birth."

The news of Maria's death hit Guido like a heavy hammer, threatening to shatter his heart. He dropped his face into his hands, and sobbed for his lost love. Beppe put his arm around Guido, not knowing what else he could do, just to let him know he was there, and Guido wasn't alone in his grief. When the tears began to subside, Guido slowly raised his head.

"I am so sorry for your loss, my son. Maria loved you very much; you were the love of her life. She often spoke fondly of you, and told us what a good man you were. She said you could always make her smile, and she loved the way you would whistle a happy tune where ever you went. From what I have been able to learn of you, Maria was correct about her impressions.

Maria named her child Rita, and gave her into our care to be raised, in the same loving environment she herself grew up in. We baptized Rita, and have raised her and loved her as if she were our own. It was not until recently that we became aware that you survived the war, but were disabled from your wounds. I didn't know if you were in a position physically to raise Rita, of if you were even willing to take responsibility for her. I decided you should at least have the opportunity to learn you had a daughter, and find out from you personally whether you wanted her or not." The mother Superior looked at Guido, who was still reeling from the shock of Maria's death, trying to gauge his reaction.

All of the Sisters that were sitting silently on the benches outside of their rooms, lining the corridors, and were all turned in the direction of the mother Superior. They were waiting, as if they were holding their breath, to see if this man who had come on the crutches would be someone who would welcome the small jewel who had become so precious to them.

"Mother, the news you have shared with me has brought me great sadness, but it has also given me peace and closure. I have been out of my mind with worry, wondering where Maria went. Sister Angelica took care of me when I was in the hospital in Trento. She gave me this cross that belonged to her own mother, and asked me to keep it with me all of my life. I have never been a religious man, I felt like God never had any interest in me. In light of what you have shared with me, I know now I was wrong. I can feel Maria here with me at this very moment, and God helped you find me so I can understand that He really does care about me. I lost half of my leg in battle, but God helped me keep my promise to bring my friend home. My friend has become my brother, and has welcomed me into his home. His wife is like a sister, and they both look out for me. Beppe and Lucia have a son, Paul, who has brought great joy into their life, and helped them heal for the effects of this terrible war. Now you tell me I too have been blessed with a child, and I thank God that He has preserved a part of my dear Maria in our daughter. It would be an honor to accept Rita into my life, and I promise you, Mother, and all of you Sisters, that I will be the best father to her as long as I live." Guido was sitting up as straight as he could manage, and smiling at all of the Nuns that were watching him from their posts. It seemed like they were breathing again, and united in a silent prayer of thanks to God for Guido's good heart.

With that the Mother Superior raised her hand, signaling the Sisters to go and get Rita. "We are so happy that you will share in the joy that has been our dear little Rita. We don't have any Grappa to celebrate this special occasion, but if you will look behind you, I think you will agree that the angel that is walking toward us is a treasure far beyond any you could hope for." The lines in the mother Superior's face transformed into a glowing smile as she reached out for the little porcelain doll walking at Sister Felice's side. She went straight into Mother's out stretched arms, as if she were accustomed to doing so. She was dressed simply, but the angels themselves would envy her beautiful green eyes and her hair that looked as if it had been spun from pure gold. She was shy, as she peeked around mother's robe at the two strange men sitting in the garden.

Guido had trouble seeing Rita for the tears streaming down his face, not daring to take his eyes off of her for fear she would vanish like a dream. Beppe kept his arm around Guido's shoulder, where it had been since they first sat down. His own tears a grateful payment to God for the blessing He had afforded his dear friend.

"My heart," mother said, smiling down at the little face that obviously adored her, "This gentleman has come a very long way to meet you." She reached out her hand to Guido, and brought Rita closer to him. Guido put his hand in mother Superiors, and waited.

"This is your father, and God has blessed us to help find him, after he has returned to us from the war. He is overjoyed to learn that you have been here with us, and he has come to take you home." Rita looked up uncertainly at the Nun, and looked back at Guido again, and smiled shyly.

"Go and give your farther a hug, my dear, he has waited so long to greet you." She took a hesitant step in his direction, and then closed the distance between them. At that point Guido could no longer restrain himself, and swept her into his arms, bathing her hair with his tears. He held her as if he would never let her go, and Rita reached up and gently patted his face.

"I am so happy to meet you, Rita; I had no idea that your mother left me with such a priceless treasure. This is your Uncle Beppe, and we will live with him in his Castle. You will be a Princess, my love, and we will all be your family. You have an Aunt Lucia, who will adore you also. Your Aunt and Uncle have a son, Paul who is your age, and will now be your brother. Your Grandmother Donna Hermenia will be overjoyed to see you, and thank God for bringing you into our lives. We will bring you back here often to visit these wonderful members of our very large family, who have loved you and cared for you." Guido beamed at his daughter, and smiled back at the nuns who could no longer hold the tears that had flooded their hearts.

"Dear Friends, the day is far spent, and it will be dark and cold soon. Would you stay and share our simple meal with us, and continue your journey in the morning? We would be so glad to spend one last night with our dear Rita, before she goes off to meet the rest of her family," mother Superior, requested, with tears standing in her own eyes.

"Of course, mother," nodded Beppe, waiting patiently for his turn to hold Rita. "We would be most grateful to accept your kind hospitality. It has been a very long and eventful day, and it is an honor to spend the evening in this peaceful and loving place with such good company."

Dawn found Guido already up and sitting in the garden, thinking about all of the things that had taken place here yesterday that had changed his life for ever. He thought of his beloved Maria, and the burden she had quietly carried in his absence. He thought of the good Sisters here, taking her in and making the last few months of her life happy ones. He thought of how they, too, had been blessed by the birth of his beautiful little girl. These women would never know the happiness of having a child of their own, but they still had been given the opportunity to be mothers in the purest sense of the word by loving her and caring for her. They had been generously repaid for their love and devotion in the eyes of a tiny angel who clearly adored each and every one of them.

Thanks to the bond of love and devotion with Beppe and his family, Guido now too had a family to present to Rita. They would love and cherish her as if she were their own, because in their hearts she would indeed be their own, just as he was. Rita would have Paul to grow up with and play with. They would explore the world around them together, and share their laughter and adventures and triumphs. He couldn't understand how he could have been so fortunate and blessed. He did know that he would not draw another breath in his life without being grateful to God for His infinite love and care.

Mother Superior joined Guido, interrupting his reveries, and sat down beside him on the bench. "I am sure this is all very overwhelming, my son, how are you feeling this morning?" the Mother Superior asked with a gentle smile.

"I was just sitting here thinking about all of the good people who have come into my life, and wondering what I ever did to deserve it. It gives me courage and hope to know that I will always be able to face whatever challenges life hands me," replied Guido, glancing down at his folded pant leg. "I am a little scared to think about taking Rita out of this place. She was born here in this beautiful, peaceful sanctuary, surrounded by people who love her and are devoted to her. The world outside those doors is a far different place, with all of the problems and discord and heart break. I can't stand the thought of her being hurt by those things; she is a perfect child who loves everyone and everything!"

"That will be your challenge as her father, to do what you can to protect her as much as you can, but still teach her to understand and deal with the things of the world that will inevitably come crashing in on her. Keep her close to God, and He will help you see your way to help her. He knows us all far better than we know ourselves, and He alone can help us, when we are lost and can't find our way." The mother reassured him, with a smile that said her words came from hard won experience. "I am sure you will be a good father to Rita, and no child will have ever been more welcomed and loved and cherished than she will be."

"Thank you for your kind words and confidence, Mother Superior, your faith in me is humbling, and I shall do my very best to live up to them." Guido smiled back at her, taking her hand, and placing a kiss in her palm out of respect for this wise and gentle woman.

Mother Superior reached into the deep pocket of her long robes, and produced a plain white envelope. She looked at it for a moment, as if she were remembering something that had given her great satisfaction and joy. "As the time grew near for Maria to give birth, she sat down at the small desk in her room and wrote a letter to you. She had no way of knowing if you were still alive, but it seemed important to her to try and communicate with you somehow." She smiled, and handed the letter to Guido, who took it with trembling hands.

He sat and stared at it in his callused hands, the last words of the woman he loved. All of the gold ever dug out of the ground, since time began, would not have been as precious to him as this thin fragile bit of paper. It would provide the miraculous means to carry the words of Maria's heart and soul to him, even though the ground had reclaimed her body. He felt an awe and reverence for it, dreading the sacrilege of tearing it open. He finally found the courage to open the letter, and began to read it out loud, never once considering it too personal not to share it with the woman who had loved and raised Maria as her own.

"My Dearest Love,

If you are ever permitted to read these words, then the fondest wish of my heart will have been granted by God, and you will have returned to us from this terrible war. I read the papers, and listen to the news, and hear from others who have had word of family and friends locked in this dreadful struggle of wills. I pray for you every day, and you are never out of my thoughts. I was so over come at the thought of you leaving me to go off to war, and never returning, that I sinned against God to quiet my fears that I would never have the opportunity to experience your love. God has punished me for my weakness and impatience and my lack of faith in Him. I am well cared for by the Sisters who were here for me, when I was unwanted by the world, and left like a bag of trash on their doorstep. I am at peace in this beautiful place, spared the harsh censure of the world for my indiscretion. I am grateful for God's mercy, but I am haunted by the ever present feeling that I *will not live to raise this child born of our love for each other. It is a great deal to ask of you, but I trust that I know you well enough that you will accept our child and love it as much as you have loved me. Know that I love you both, and I will never be far away from either of you. I will watch over you from what ever heaven I am permitted to enter, knowing God's love will never punish a child for the sins of her parents. I pray that you forgive me for this burden I have placed on you.*

Know that I have loved you with all of my heart. I remain eternally yours,

Maria

Guido bowed his head, holding the scrap to his chest, as if his heart would break. How could she believe that he wouldn't want this living reminder of her, and the symbol of their love?

"I am glad she had the opportunity to tell you how she felt, and the things that were in her heart. I feel certain she will keep her promise to look after you and Rita. We will always include you in our prayers, and be grateful that we were blessed to have you in our lives. We will look forward to your visits, and we will write and keep in touch." The Mother Superior placed her hand on Guido's, to emphasize their unfailing support for them. She turned at the sound of a door opening, and smiled fondly to see Rita approaching them with a small suitcase in one hand, and her favorite doll clutched tightly to her chest.

As if responding to some silent signal that only they could hear, the doors of the corridors began to open, and the Sisters emerged, coming to say their good byes. Rita was surrounded by a sea of black and white, as each Nun in her turn, held Rita. They whispered their farewells in her small ear, hugging her and kissing her, before handing her over to the next set of out stretched arms.

Beppe brought the car up to the front door of the convent, and prepared to load his precious cargo. Guido emerged from the door, accompanied by Rita holding on to one of his crutches with her small hand, and mother carrying the small suitcase that possessed the sum total of her earthly possessions. They were followed by the entire population of the Order. Beppe came and picked Rita up in his arms, and she smiled shyly at him, touching his face with her fingers. The Mother Superior held her place at the top of the steps, while the Sisters spilled out around her, each finding a place to wave her final good bye.

"I can never even begin to repay all of you for your love and kindness to Maria and Rita. All I can do is to struggle to do half as good of a job of loving Rita and raising her as you have done." Guido called, as Beppe took Rita and set her on the front seat of the car between them. Guido swung into the seat with some effort, and Beppe put his crutches in the back behind them.

"We will ask God for His choicest blessings on your family every day, and look forward to the day when we will see you again!" mother raised her hand as the car drove away from the Convent, with the Sisters waving and calling out their final blessings until the car was out of sight. Rita was sitting on Guido's lap, taking in the sights and sounds of a world she never knew existed. Guido spoke softly to her, as he pointed out the everyday marvels, and gently stroked her hair.

Chapter Six

Rita's head was constantly turning to take in the wonders before her. The engine of the great car hummed as it carried them in comfort to their destination. The majestic mountains with their robes of snow passed the windows, as they sparkled in the morning sun. The horses, cows, sheep and goats, grazing in the fields, lifted curious heads as the car passed them. The panoramic scenes, with the quaint little houses dotting the mountain slopes that spread before them on their journey home, were breathtaking. It reminded Beppe of something he had seen as a boy in a beautiful Nativity Scene, set up for Christmas in a big cathedral.

Rita loved it when Uncle Beppe would honk the horn at people they passed working in the fields, laughing in pure delight. She would anticipate their friendly waves, and point out new prospects they could greet, in this most entertaining method, with a squeal of joy. Beppe, for his part, loved hearing the new title that had been bestowed upon him, making his formal title of Count seem tired and ordinary by comparison. "Bip, Bip, Bip," Rita would call out, pointing excitedly at some new wonder. The two men laughed right along with her, becoming boys again as they saw the world fresh and new, through her wondering eyes.

The long hours of the trip home seemed to evaporate; they were both entranced watching Rita reacting to a world that amazed her at every turn. As the car approached the outskirts of Lake Braies, Beppe kept up a steady beep of the loud horn, to announce their arrival home. The tall pine trees lining the road acted as tall green sentinels, like an honor guard of soldiers welcoming home a returning Queen. The people of the town looked back at them, waving at the familiar car, and wondering if Beppe and Guido had lost their senses.

As the car neared the Castle, Beppe took up his honking again, to alert everyone on the Estate that they were home. He was so excited to be bringing them this unexpected and exciting news. He continued to drive round and round the stately fountain at the entrance to the Castle, honking his horn and kicking up the loose gravel of the driveway. Everyone came running out, wondering if some familiar Alpini had deprived the tavern of their last drop of wine. All of the gardeners and maids and servants gathered near the front steps to see what all of the commotion was about. Donna Lucia and Paul appeared at the top of the stairs, with wonder and confusion on their faces from this most unusual display by Beppe.

Beppe finally stopped the car near the stairs, and hurried around the car to open the door for Guido and

Rita. He handed Guido his crutches, and picked up Rita in his arms, like a conquering hero returning home with his treasure.

"Ladies and Gentlemen, friends all," announced Beppe as the assembled group looked on in amazement, "I have the most miraculous news to share with you! This is Guido's daughter, Rita. We just learned about this great blessing yesterday, and she will become a part of our extended family and bless us with her beautiful soul."

With that Lucia rushed down the stairs to greet her new niece, and knelt down so Rita, now standing on the ground and holding Guido's hand could look at her face to face. Rita smiled, looking into the face of her new Aunt, and grabbed her around the neck. Lucia hugged her back, holding a daughter she had longed for, with tears streaming down her face. Paul had followed her, not quite able to understand what all of this could mean.

"My son, God has been very good to us. This is your Uncle Guido's daughter, Rita. She will be like a sister to you, and the two of you will be the best of friends." Lucia pulled her confused son closer. Paul, to his credit, reached down and picked up the small doll that had slipped from Rita's grasp as she greeted Lucia. He handed it to Rita, and smiled with real joy at the news of his unexpected good fortune. He would now have someone to explore the gardens with, and share all of the secrets Uncle Guido had taught him about the beautiful flowers that he helped grow.

Guido stood watching as everyone he knew came closer to give a welcome to this small gift from God. The tears that ran down his face, unchecked, were the tears of a man who had been given a second chance at life. The horrors of the terrible war he had endured, and the pain and sacrifices he had experienced, seemed to fade on the steps of the Castle in the warmth of the sun on an afternoon that would forever live in his heart. He was so grateful for the open and loving welcome to this tiny little girl. He was sure Maria was nearby, weeping for joy at their daughter's reception. From their excited expressions he could see that no one gave a thought to the scandal that had been uppermost in Maria's mind when she had quietly fled her life and friends in Lake Braies, and sought the safety of the convent. The Donat family was truly of noble birth, but it was nobility that extended far beyond their estate and titles. They were possessed of a kind and generous heart that knew no boundaries. Rita was genuinely a member of this great family in every way that mattered, and nothing would ever change that.

As peace and harmony descended on the Castle, the practical matters of getting Rita settled in came into view. Guido would require help caring for Rita, because of his crutches and his difficulty in getting around. Lucia's assistant Nina had been a good and faithful friend to her over the years, seeing her though her most trying times. Nina was a good woman and loved children dearly, even though she had never married and had any children of her own. She was a very religious person, and found joy in helping to raise Paul and every other child of her acquaintance. Nina was delighted with the assignment to help Guido with Rita.

The next day Donna Lucia, Nina, and Rita went into the town to find some new clothes for Rita. Every where they went they were greeted by the people of Lake Braies, who wanted to meet the daughter of the town's hero. Rita was mystified by all of these strange new people, but she charmed them all with her shy smile, and her winning ways.

Nina, for her part, was the happiest person anywhere. She understood the feelings of the Sisters of the Convent, who filled the empty holes in their lives by being allowed to raise Rita. Some thoughtless people would call Nina a spinster, and dismiss her as less than a real woman because she had no children. Nina couldn't have cared less about their narrow opinions of her. She was indeed a mother because she helped Rita and Paul grow and flourish. Every day was a joy to her, and she never gave a second thought to those who pitied or looked down on her. Nina didn't have much of a formal education, but she loved sharing the bits of wisdom and experience with Rita and Paul that she had gleaned over the years.

Donna Lucia was concerned that she had put too much on Nina, charging her with taking charge of Rita, and helping Guido too. One evening after dinner, while Guido and Beppe were enjoying their pipes and a glass of Grappa, she talked to Nina about her concerns.

"Nina, you work so hard around here taking care of Rita, and all of the other things you have to attend to. I was wondering if you might know of a good woman in the town who could help you with Rita, and take some of the load off of your shoulders." Lucia looked at her friend with real fondness and concern in her eyes.

"I can't imagine an easier job, and a more pleasant way of spending my day than looking after Rita and Guido. I appreciate the opportunity that has been mine, and I couldn't be happier. I have been concerned that I don't have as much education as I should have had, because I can't teach Rita all of the things she should know. I know of a widow in Lake Braies, Mrs. Anna Carbone, who lost her husband in the war. They never had any children, and she loves children as much as I do. She has a good education, and has a lot of knowledge that I missed out on. She is about your age, Guido; did you know her in school?" Nina looked over at Guido and Beppe who had been listening in on the conversation.

"Yes" replied Guido, "I do remember her. Beppe and I knew her husband in the army; he was a very good man and a good soldier."

Beppe nodded at what Guido had said, "He was a very good Alpini, but he wasn't as lucky or as fortunate as us. We were taken care of by the very hand of God Himself. It would be a good thing if we were to assist his dear wife, by hiring her to help with Rita and Guido. I am sure her husband would approve, and we would be repaying, in a very small way, a debt we owe to so many good men who can't be here to provide for their families any more." Beppe smiled over at his friend, and could tell that he agreed with everything that he had just said.

"Tomorrow is the market fair in town. Beppe, would you like to talk to Mrs. Anna Carbone, and see if she would agree to such an arrangement?" Guido asked Beppe, remembering their shopping trip.

"That is a great idea! We will take the children and the carriage and make a day of it. Rita and Paul will have a good time helping us with our chores, and Mrs. Carbone will get to meet them. They will do our work for us; and convince her to take the job. Who could say no to those two faces?" Beppe laughed, clearly amused by his scheme to secure a new member for their family.

Chapter Seven

The next morning everyone headed to town in the carriage, excited to go to the market fair. There were so many good things to eat, and wonderful smells filled the air from all of the venders selling their wares. They finally headed for Mrs. Carbone's home, and after the carriage came to a stop, Beppe got out and came around and helped Guido get out, just like he always did. They knocked on the door, but there was no answer. Her apartment was across the narrow street from Guido's small flower shop and apartment. He had lived there before the war.

Guido crossed the street, and slowly took the keys to the door out of his pocket, and put the key in the lock and turned it. He had not been back to his former home since he left for war, and it was dusty and dark inside. He went inside, and looked around, remembering happier times in this place. He sat down on a nearby chair, and closed his eyes, lost in his happy thoughts. He wasn't capable of climbing the stairs to his small bedroom, but every detail was still crystal clear in his mind. He thought with reverence of the last night he spent here, with his dear

Maria, instead of joining his friends down at the tavern. It was a memory he would treasure until his eyes closed for the last time. It was entirely possible that his jewel, Rita, began her life's journey in that small room at the top of those stairs.

Guido shook himself mentally, remembering that he had business to take care of, and got to his feet. He made his way out of the room, and closed and locked the door behind him. Beppe and the children had found something interesting to keep their attention in the small neat garden nearby.

Guido knocked at the door again, and this time the door opened. He was met by a stately woman, with her hair pulled back and kept in place by beautiful silver combs. Upon recognizing her caller she said "Well, for heaven's sake, Guido Marron, is that really you?"

"Good morning Mrs. Carbone, I am glad you still remember me, it has been a very long time. Hopefully the war didn't change me too much," laughed Guido, with an apologetic glance down at his leg.

"How can I forget you? I have known you forever. It sounds ridiculous for you to call me Mrs. Carbone; I am just Anna to you. Won't you come in a share a glass of good wine with me? How have you been?" Anna replied with a gesture of her hand to come inside.

"Thank you Anna, I am still alive!" Guido thought about what he usually said to those he was used to teasing with. His eyes were huge with shock as he thought about how it might sound to someone whose husband died in the war.

Anna saw the look on his face and just laughed. "Don't worry about it Alpino, every one has their own destiny. My dear husband was proud to serve his country." Another older woman entered the room, and nodded politely to Guido. "This is my mother, Mrs. Delia-—she probably remembers you too."

"Of course I remember the little boy who used to pull your pigtails when you were in school. It is good to see you, Sergeant Marron, the whole town is so proud of you." The older woman was very glad to be able to express her feelings about Guido's heroism.

'Thank you Mrs. Delia, there are a great many brave men from Lake Braies, I am just fortunate to be able to return home. The medals belong to those who didn't come home." Guido said, always modest about his part in the war.

"Tell me, what brings you to my doorstep today?" Anna poured a glass of wine for Guido and her mother, as well as one for herself, before she sat down across from their guest.

"Since I returned from the war I have lived with Beppe and his good wife Donna Lucia at the Castle. They have become my family, and I am a very fortunate man to have such good and loving friends. I love bringing the gardens back to life, and making things beautiful around the Estate again." Guido started out, to tell them about his errand.

"I have seen the beautiful flowers and trees, but I don't think you have come to discuss gardening with me today." Anna added, smiling at her friend.

"No, no, of course not, you are right." Guido took the last sip of wine from his glass, and straightened his shoulders and looked her straight in the eyes. "Not long ago I received a letter from Udine, asking me to come on some unspecified business. I was intrigued, as I knew no one in that city, and couldn't imagine what they wanted. Beppe and I decided to drive up there and satisfy our curiosity about this mysterious letter. It turned out to be a convent, and they had a story to share with me." Guido paused, looking at Anna. She just looked back at him, waiting to hear about the mystery, so he continued.

"You may remember Maria, the maid who worked for Dr. Marron and his family for a few years. She was a very nice young woman, and we were seeing each other, before I went off to war with the other Alpini. Maria was raised at that convent, and the mother Superior is Dr. Marron's cousin. That is how Maria came to work for them when she decided not to become a nun and join their order. After I left, Maria disappeared. I couldn't find out what happened to her after I got out of the hospital and came home to Lake Braies. It turns out that Maria went back to the convent, to live with the Sisters who raised her." Guido paused again, uncertain about continuing. Anna just nodded, encouraging him to go on.

"I didn't know that Maria was pregnant, and she was ashamed, and didn't know where to turn. She went back to the only home she had ever known, to have our baby. I don't have to explain to you why she was so afraid I might never return. Maria had a hard time with the birth, and died when our daughter was born. I was shocked and saddened to learn of her passing. The Sisters just found out that I had survived, and asked me to come to the convent, to see for themselves how I felt about having a child. They weren't certain I would want her. I was overjoyed to have the blessing of a beautiful daughter in my life, so Beppe and I brought her home. The family has taken her to their hearts, just like they did me. Donna Lucia's assistant, Nina, has been helping me to care for Rita, but we are thinking she could use some help. You are a well educated woman, Anna, and we were hoping you might consider coming to the Castle and helping us care for her." Guido held his breath, the last few words of his request coming out like a gust of wind.

Anna laughed and said, "Only taking care of Rita? You don't have to look so serious, my friend. These streets are very narrow, and the windows have very big eyes. Everyone knows about dear sweet Maria, now, and the miracle that you brought back from Udine. We knew Maria well, and she would visit Mother and me often and we would talk and catch up on all of the news of our little town. I was concerned when she left town without a word to any body, or even a goodbye. There are some that would judge her, but she should have known that we would not be among them. We are so relieved to finally learn the truth." Anna looked at her mother, and she nodded firmly that she agreed with everything that Anna had said.

Guido smiled back at his childhood friend, with relief and gratitude for her words of understanding. At that moment they both heard the sound of hoofs on the cobblestones outside, and they knew the Beppe had returned with the carriage to collect Guido. "That will be Beppe; he took the children for a ride, so that I could talk with you. Would you like to come outside and meet his son Paul, and my dear little Rita?"

"What a silly question!" Anna followed Guido to the front steps and called out, "Good evening Count Donat, children, please come in and I will make you some hot chocolate."

"Thank you Mrs. Carbone, we would appreciate some hot chocolate very much!" called Beppe from the carriage, and looked behind him to see Paul and Rita clapping their hands together in delight.

Anna was pleased to see such well mannered children, but she was surprised when Rita approached her shyly to speak to her. "What is it, my dear? You can tell me anything."

Rita glanced back at her uncle and her father and her cousin, a little hesitant to say what was on her mind. Finally she decided, and inched a little closer to Anna, reaching up gently to touch her hair. "You have such beautiful hair Madame."

"Why thank you my dear, you have the most beautiful eyes. What is your name?" Anna already knew her name, but she wanted to give the shy little girl an opportunity to say a little more.

"My name is Rita," she went on confidently, sure of her answer, "And this is my cousin Paul."

The children returned to their hot chocolate, and Beppe turned to look outside. "It will be getting dark soon, we should be going. I hope you will accept our sincere offer to come and help us care for Rita. I promise you will be like one of our family, and you will be very happy living at the Castle with us. In our home there is no Count and Countess, it is just Beppe and Lucia and Guido. You will have to put up with a couple of old Alpinos, but perhaps that will be a good thing and you will feel closer to your own Alpino who is no longer with us."

Guido attempted to get up, but he had been sitting for a while, and he was embarrassed when he was unable to get to his feet on the first try. Anna automatically reached down and helped him, but he was ashamed that he couldn't do it himself. "You don't have to be that way with your friends, Alpino! Be grateful to God that you have lived to see another beautiful day. I would give anything to help my husband get to his feet; I would pay any price to be able to do that small service for him!" Anna scolded, in mock anger, relieving Guido's mind.

Beppe kissed Anna's hand, and said "I know we have given you a great deal to consider, this would be a big change in your quiet life. We will wait for your answer, hoping that you will say yes."

Looking at the faces of the children, and these two earnest men, made Anna's decision easy. "You won't have to wait for an answer, I would be honored to be counted among your wonderful family and come and help care for Rita and Guido. It will take me a few days to organize myself, but I will be along as soon as I can."

The following Sunday Anna's uncle drove her to the Castle early in the morning, with all of the things she thought she would need loaded in the back of his wagon. Anna looked all around her at this idyllic setting, with only the sound of the fountain and the singing of the birds breaking the silence of the moment.

"You must be Anna," greets Nina, coming around the corner of the Castle with a big bouquet of flowers in her hands destined for the front entryway.

"Yes I am," answered Anna, "Do you know me?"

"I should say I do! I have known you since you were a little girl, I knew your mother very well. I used to see her frequently when I lived in town. I am so glad you have come to live with us; this is a very special place with special people. I adore the children, it is great to be around them and hear their laughter and see the world again through their eyes. I am not as young as I used to be, so it will be a great help to me to have you here to share my work. This will be wonderful, and I promise you will be as happy here as I have been."

"Where is everyone?" asked Anna, looking around her.

"They are in church; we have our own chapel here at the Castle. It is a separate building, just around the corner. If you would like to attend Mass with them, just leave your belongings here, they will be safe." invited Nina with a reassuring smile. Anna nodded in return, and headed off in the direction that Nina had indicated.

The chapel was picturesque, and looked like it was built about the same time as the Castle. It must have been important to the original owners, who constructed this place, to include a chapel in their plans. Their faith must have been as important to them as having a roof over their heads. Anna stopped at the entrance to the chapel, and removed a small black scarf from her purse, and placed it on her head, before taking a seat in the back. She was amazed at how many people were scattered throughout the carved wooden pews. It was gratifying to see that there didn't seem to be any order as to how the people who were attending the Mass were seated. As the service ended, because she was closest to the door, she was the first to emerge, waiting patiently for some familiar faces to make their way out into the morning sunshine.

Anna recognized some of the maids and gardeners and the household staff. Some of them she hadn't realized worked on the Estate, others she did. They all greeted her with calls of recognition, and smiles and hugs. They were glad she would be joining their family here, and they all referred to it as such. She was just beginning to talk with the priest, when she heard Rita's familiar voice behind her.

"Anna, Anna, you came!" shouted Rita, as she scampered through the crowd to reach Anna. Everyone smiled and made a path for Rita, as she launched herself into Anna's outstretched arms.

"My, I believe you have grown an inch since I saw you last week! If this keeps up, you will have to be holding me soon," laughed Anna, hugging Rita tightly.

Guido just stood there on his crutches, next to Beppe and Lucia, as they shared the joyous reunion together on this beautiful warm morning. The birds joined in the chorus of contentment, accompanied by the humming of the bees and the soft breeze.

Beppe was the first to reach Anna. "Anna, we are delighted to finally have you here with us, the children have been watching the driveway every day, impatiently waiting for your arrival. We were afraid they would try and sleep on the steps to make sure they were here the moment you came into view! May I introduce my wife, Lucia? She has been almost as anxious as Guido and the children."

"It is so good to finally meet you, Anna," replied Donna Lucia, reaching out to embrace Anna as if she were her long lost sister. "Nina has told me so much about you that I feel we are already the best of friends. I hope you will feel at home with us right away, and be happy here for all of the years ahead of us!"

"You are so kind," answered Anna, returning her embrace. "Your husband and Guido said that I would feel like family if I agreed to come and care for Rita. I can see that they were absolutely right. Since my husband's death I have gotten along well enough, but I have missed the feeling of belonging to a larger family. I can't tell you how much this means to me to be here in this lovely place, and feel like I have finally come home. I see that it is true when God closes a door; he opens up a window in heaven and pours out a blessing so large that there is not enough room to contain it. Thank you for this opportunity not only to earn a living. I need to be part of something greater than myself, and feel the peace and contentment that I have been missing in my life. I will be honored to help in whatever way I can. You have a wonderful son, Lucia, and he and Rita are a great credit to you. I could see the love and patience they have been raised with, they are so polite and caring. Raising them will be a joy."

Guido finally made his way over to the crowd gathered around Anna, slowly on his crutches. His heart was full, that his childhood friend had accepted Beppe and Lucia's gracious offer to come and help with caring for them. He couldn't think of any more words to add; all of the loving words that had already been spoken. He just offered his own sincere "Thank-you, Anna, welcome to our home," looking her straight in the eyes.

Beppe slapped Guido on the back and retorted, "Well, we surely have a full house! Let's go see about some lunch."

Chapter Eight

As the group neared the entrance of the Castle, Anna detoured over to pick up her bags and take them inside. "No," called out Beppe, "Let us help you with those heavy bags. Nicola, would you give us a hand with the luggage? If you need anything, Nicola and Nina will see that it will be taken care of."

As they entered the foyer of the Castle, Anna was shocked into silence by what she saw. She was a simple person from a simple family. She had never seen such opulence and beauty in her entire life. The interior was something out of a story book, with its marble floors and gleaming wood work. The staircase commanded attention, as soon as one walked in the front door, and the huge round table was a stunning backdrop for the fresh flowers that must be brought in each day from the gardens. There were pictures, tapestries, and statues lining the walls, and the crystal chandeliers gave the whole room the appearance of a fairytale.

"Your home is lovely, Count Donat," Anna finally managed to get out, still amazed by the sights surrounding her.

"Beppe, please Anna, we don't stand on ceremony here. I am pleased you like our home. Each one of my ancestors added something to the Castle when they lived here. I hope we will leave a lasting legacy for our children. You will get used to it soon enough, and it will become home to you." Beppe smiled reassuringly at her.

"Shall we go in and eat?" asked Donna Lucia. "Conversation is always more pleasant over a meal." Everyone nodded in agreement, and headed for the large dining room down the hall.

After lunch, everyone made their way over to Guido's residence, adjacent to the Castle. It was a beautiful little chalet, and was very comfortable. It must have been initially built for visiting dignitaries to the Castle, who required their own residence. Guido's room was on the first floor, because he couldn't negotiate the stairs on his crutches. The rest of the living areas were on the upper floor.

"Why, this is marvelous!" exclaimed Anna, looking around in amazement for the second time in as many hours. "I can't imagine a more comfortable and inviting home. I shall feel right at home with such comfortable accommodations and wonderful people about all of the time. Count, oh I am sorry! It will take a little getting used to for me to automatically call you by your first names. Let me try again, Beppe and Donna Lucia! There, that sounded much better, didn't it?" Anna added with a shy smile.

"You will master it in no time, my dear!" assured Lucia, with a confident nod. "We will become the best of friends, and the sound of royal titles will sound odd to you before you know it!" They all laughed, knowing her statement was true enough.

"We have fixed up two of the rooms upstairs for you and Rita. I, of course will be living down here, because it isn't possible for me to make it up the stairs." Guido's voiced trailed off, as he looked down at his empty pant leg with some embarrassment showing on his face.

"Sergeant Guido Marron," said Anna in a sharp retort. "I told you when you visited me at my home that you should be grateful to God that you came back to us alive. Your leg is a minor inconvenience, and you are still able to walk and move according to your own will. You have no need to be ashamed of the price you had to pay for preserving your life! You have a wonderful daughter and a family who loves you. Many people go to bed every night praying to God for even one of your many blessings!"

"I am sorry, Anna," replied Guido, with a look of a small boy who had just gotten a good scolding. "Of course you are right. There are many of my friends who only have a small white cross to mark their residence on a mountain top far from their loved ones. I promise you I won't be making a habit of feeling sorry for myself." Guido stood a little taller, with his crutches, as if to emphasize his resolve.

Turning to Rita and Paul, with a renewed smile on her face Anna said, "Well, young ones, are you as happy to have me here to be your friend and helper, as I am to be here?"

"Yes!" Rita and Paul chorused together as if they had rehearsed it for long hours. They both hugged Anna, and smiled up at her with excitement clearly written on their faces.

"It will be important that you learn to follow my instructions, so we can get all of the wonderful things that we have planned done. I would like us to go to the chapel together every morning, to thank God for our many blessings. Your fathers are so fortunate to come home to Lake Braies and be a part of your lives. So many of our brave Alpini were not so fortunate, and we will pray for their families that they will learn to cope with their absence. Then we will go outside into the garden and play and enjoy the beautiful flowers. I have a surprise for both of you!" Anna said, with a sweet smile, as she was opening one of her trunks.

Paul and Rita were instantly at her side, peering into the trunk, hoping for a first glimpse at what might be inside. Anna pulled out the first surprise, wrapped in white tissue paper and handed it to Rita, and the second tissue-clad surprise she handed to Paul. Each child glowed with excitement, tearing the paper off to see what was inside.

"Oh," squealed Rita in delight, upon spying her gift. "She is the most beautiful dolly I have ever had, I shall love her forever!" Rita beamed at Anna, cradling her new treasure in her arms.

"It's a car that can run around the floor, all by itself," announced Paul,

Expertly winding it up and letting it go. It raced across the floor, like a flash, and disappeared under a chair before it ran out of energy. "Thank you Anna, I love it! It will be fun to see how far it can go down the big hall outside my bedroom. I'll bet it can make it all of the way to the stairs!" Paul was already running across the room, to discover what had become of his new marvel.

Guido took in the happy scene with real peace and contentment. He started to feel more like the young man who boarded a train in Lake Braies with the other Alpini, eager for the big adventure that lay ahead. Perhaps he hoped that there might be a special relationship develop someday with his childhood friend. He was still a handsome young man with a lot of good years ahead of him.

Later that evening, Anna was very candid about her feelings about sharing his home. "Guido, we were friends as children, and we even dated some when we were older. I want you to understand that I am here to help raise and care for Rita and Paul. It will be my pleasure to assist you with whatever I can to make your days more manageable, but I am not interested in you personally."

"Of course, Anna," replied Guido, with a smile that he did not feel. "I am so grateful that you have come to help us. You have so much to offer the children, both as a teacher and a friend. Your presence will make this house a home, and your laughter and bright smile will help erase some of the loss we have all experienced."

Perhaps in the years to come, Anna would grow to have a deeper relationship with Guido, as she spent more time with him. She was still grieving for the loss of her dear husband. She might eventually turn to him because of their shared loss of the people who filled their lives. For now, he would be content with the care and companionship of an old friend, someone who Rita could pattern her life after.

Chapter Nine

Beppe and Donna Lucia grew to love Anna from the moment she came to live in the Castle, and become part of their large extended family. Both Rita and Paul doted on Anna, and followed her eagerly where ever she went. They polished their manners and behavior under her gentle tutelage. She read stories to them, and helped them to start exploring their world. She would recount the history of Lake Braies, acquainting them with their proud heritage. They would roam the Estate together, learning about the trees and bushes and flowers. They would help Guido with his flowers, and assist cutting and bringing them to Nina to make the rooms in the Castle sing with the song of the garden.

Paul and Rita grew, and Guido swore he could stand there and watch them get taller. He, Beppe, Donna Lucia, and Anna discussed the children's education. They could well afford to send them to the finest schools, but they would be away from friends and family. It was decided that they should attend the local school, and develop lasting friendships with the children they would meet in school. It was important to Beppe and Donna Lucia that

Paul and Rita grew up to appreciate everyone they came into contact with. They didn't want them to grow up to be spoiled and selfish, believing themselves somehow better than others because of their background.

In addition to attending public school, Paul and Rita would also have special tutors and additional work at home to help them reach their potentials and dreams. Anna would take Paul and Rita to school every morning, and then go to visit her mother or run errands for the family while she waited for school to conclude for the day. She shared with her mother her life in the Castle, and all of the special moments that she spent with the children. Her mother was happy to see that Anna was able to smile again, after the devastating blow from her husband's death. Anna spoke of Guido often and his cheerful nature as he worked to bring the Estate's gardens back to their former glory. She was genuinely fond of Guido, and admired him for his good and caring heart. It was difficult to judge him harshly when he was clearly such a hero to everyone on the Estate.

Beppe and Donna Lucia were doing well in restoring the Estate to the prosperity that it enjoyed before the war. The farms were doing very well, and the weather had been very favorable to help produce bountiful harvests. The livestock was expanding and flourishing, with new breeds improving their quality of stock. Meat, milk, and eggs had been in such short supply during the war that there was a market begging for every pound of meat, and eggs, and cheese, and milk that they could produce. Ever grateful for their blessings and prosperity, Beppe and Donna Lucia made the contribution of an addition to the local hospital in Lake Braies as their legacy. With assistance from the banks, and funds from the region of Venezia Giulia, they were able to add on an entire new wing.

Children had always had a special place in their hearts. The new wing was dedicated to helping children with infectious diseases as well as respiratory problems like asthma. They also founded a special training program for specialized nursing, as well as training for paramedics to aide in responding to accidents and emergency situations. It elevated the town of Lake Braies to a very important place for medical treatment, and set the standard for hospitals in the entire region.

It seemed times of great happiness and contentment are usually balanced by sadness and heartbreak. After years of declining health, Countess Hermenia, Beppe's noble mother, finally passed away. When the end came for her, she was surrounded by her family and friends. Her grandchildren were her greatest prize, and Paul and Rita were next to her on the bed when she bid them her final farewell. She adored both Paul and Rita, and made no distinction between them. Paul, as he grew, looked more and more like her dear husband, Francesco. The resemblance between the two of them was remarkable. Rita would always bring her fresh flowers for her room, and loved to hear tales of the Castle and those who had called it home.

Beppe would now be Count Giuseppe Donat, the hereditary heir of the lands and title. He was sad that God had only blessed him and Lucia with one child, but in truth, Rita was as much his daughter as if she had been born to them. He hoped that Paul would grow up to be a good man, and extend the families descendants well into the future.

Paul was a credit to his father, and his uncle Guido. He was loved by all who knew him. He had a quick mind, and was curious about everything around him. He was kind and thoughtful, and loved working in the garden with Guido, soaking up his wisdom and experience. He and Rita were the best of friends, and they seldom saw one without the other.

Rita was growing into a beautiful young woman, and had a real zest for life. Everything was an adventure, and she could run and play all day, or sit quietly for hours watching a butterfly free itself from its cocoon. She loved to read, and listen to her father talk about her mother and what a wonderful person she was. A favorite outing of hers was going with Anna into town to do some shopping. She and Paul liked to visit with all of the sellers and catch up on the news of the area. The best days were the market fairs, because there were always a lot of other kids from the outlying farms that came into town. It was a good excuse to run and play and have fun, while still doing the errands for the Estate. She and Paul loved going with Anna to visit Anna's mother. They loved her and called her "Grandma Delia". The older woman was delighted to see the children, and considered them the grandchildren she had so longed for.

Anna enjoyed caring for Rita and Paul and Guido. There was a predictable routine to her life that was safe and comforting. She still kept her emotional distance from Guido, preferring to think of him as a good friend or a brother. Her husband had been the love of her life, and it was unthinkable in her mind that anyone could take his place. It was her own mother that broached the subject of Guido with her on one of their frequent visits.

"Anna, my dear," ventured Mrs. Delia during tea one afternoon, "Am I wrong to think that you might be experiencing more that just friendship for Guido? You always speak so highly of him as a father and a friend. Is there anything more than that in your heart, my daughter?"

"Why would you ask me such a thing? There has only been one man in my life, and I still cry sometimes when I wake up in the mornings and find that he is not here," answered Anna, with apparent distress clearly written on her face.

"Your husband would be unhappy if he thought you were still grieving for him, after all of these years. He loved you so, and he would want you to be happy. Guido is a good and honorable man and Alpini too. I have seen how he looks at you, with fondness and respect when he comes to town with Beppe and the children," her mother observed, taking another sip from her cup.

"You are right, mother; he is a very good man. When I first went to work at the Castle, I was very frank with him about my feelings. If he ever had any notion about me in that respect, I am sure my words were clear enough that he saw the futility of it a long time ago." Anna noted with a sad smile.

"My dear daughter, you are not so young any more. The things that were important to you as a young woman are less important now. If your words closed the gate to his heart, then I am sure your words could open it up again. He has had some terrible events in his life, and he has borne them with patience, whistling, and a cheerful smile. In that house there are many people who adore you, without question or reservation. Perhaps it is time to bring down the walls you have been hiding behind, and meet the world again head on." Mrs. Delia gently encouraged.

"Perhaps you are right, mother. It is something to consider." Anna got up to go, with a lot of things racing around in her head, and she wasn't sure what to make of them.

Mrs. Delia, knowing that Anna was confused and didn't like to show weakness to those around her, wrote a letter to Donna Lucia. She shared her thoughts with her, and asked for her help to break the ice between Anna and Guido. Two women can be more effective than the greatest army when it comes to matters of the heart. The two worked in concert with each other, to help Guido and Anna build a door in the wall that separated them. There were dinner parties, and family outings and special errands. They left no stone unturned to create the right atmosphere to help these two lonely people see the possibilities in each other. In a matter of a few months, they won the victory they had sought, and Guido and Anna were married in the chapel on the Estate.

It would not be the same as their first loves, with a heart of racing passion that could eclipse the sun. It was the quiet, solid love of mutual respect and devotion that would be a comfort to them both. It was someone to walk with, and talk with, and enjoy a pleasant evening with on the porch. It was having someone to button a button you couldn't reach, or help you retrieve something just beyond your fingertips on a high shelf. It was a comforting presence in the bed late at night, when you were awakened by a bad dream.

Paul and Rita entered their teenage years, well on their way to becoming the kind of person every parent could be proud of. They worked very hard in school and achieved top rankings in their respective classes. As a reward for their dedicated study, they each received a horse to help them enjoy the freedom of their summer vacation. Rita's horse was called Bianco, because he was white from nose to tail. Paul's horse was brown with white spots, and loved to jump. He called him Aries, for the Greek god of war. They rode from dawn to dusk, and crisscrossed the Estate a dozen times a day. The people of the town would see them riding past, and wave and call their greetings. It was a time of innocence, and joy. They were brother and sister, and the temptations of the world were far from their minds for now.

The stock market crash was a great financial upheaval that sent shock waves all over the world. Many of the Americans who had been in Italy since the war, helping them to rebuild and recover would now have to go home. The financial base that allowed them to help others less fortunate than themselves was gone, and they had to go home to help their own country climb the steep hill of recovery.

Rita and Paul enjoyed simple entertainments. There were plays and musical events and concerts in town, and their favorite, motion pictures. It was like a window on the world, and a small admission could take you anywhere, and give you experiences you would never find at home. It seemed like the Americans had returned when they watched John Wayne, Gary Cooper, and Fred Astaire and Ginger Rogers. It helped America find her place in the sun again, bolstered by the strength of immigrants from all over the world.

Chapter Ten

When the sun shines too long, there are always clouds to block the pleasant warm rays, and cast the world back into darkness. It seems the universal law of greed and the desire for limitless power was preparing to raise its evil head again. Adolph Hitler, with his gift for oration and his magical ability to inspire a defeated nation, cast a long shadow. Franco darkened the hopes of Spain, while the Italian people were mesmerized by Benito Mussolini. Out in the Pacific, the Japanese prepared to seek their share of the world's attention behind Emperor Hirohito.

The initial surge was good for Italy, resulting in a flurry of building activity. There were new roads and buildings and schools and hospitals. The nation had a new feeling of unity and pride, but the price they would have to pay was not far over the horizon.

However, peace and tranquility still reigned supreme in the mountains of Lake Braies, and the Castle of the Donat family was the center of the town's prosperity. But with the events taking place in the far flung reaches of the world, there was doubt and fear starting to rear its ugly head. Rita and Paul were no longer fun loving teenagers, whose biggest care was studying for a math test or seeing to it that the horses are getting regular exercise. The unrest they read about in the papers caused them to reflect on their perfect life at the Castle. They hadn't been born yet the last time war reached out to extract its terrible toll on the people of these mountains. The evidence was there in the graveyard, and the small white makers that swept the mountain sides, and in the slow gait of Guido as he made his rounds on his crutches.

Paul had reached a time in his life when the sister he grew up with and explored the fields with, was starting to take on new meaning for him. He was becoming more aware of her as a young woman, and it was confusing and troubling to him. He loved her with the respect of a brother, but he couldn't shake the feelings she evoked in him when they were together. On a beautiful Sunday afternoon ride through the Estate, far from the trouble of the world, Paul and Rita were enjoying the day. Paul was troubled, and his horse picked up on his rider's mood. Aries was edgy, and slow to take the jumps on a favorite trail he had taken a hundred times before. Paul got off, and took a look at Aries foot, looking for the reason for his hesitant stride.

"Is everything OK?" asked Rita, circling back around to see if Paul needed help.

"I was just checking Aries' foot, he didn't act right over that last jump, but I can't see anything in his hoof," replied Paul, looking up at Rita. The sight of her in the morning sun, with the wind in her hair almost swept him away, and he sat down on the old stone fence to gather up his nerve.

"Are you all right Paul, you look flushed and you're sweating." Rita dismounted, and came to sit next to Paul on the fence.

"There is something I have wanted to talk to you about for a while now, but I can't seem to come up with the right words," Paul looked at Rita, trying to get the courage to go on.

"We have known each other since we were babies; I can't imagine that there is anything that you could say to me that I wouldn't understand." Rita smiled at him, inviting him to get whatever was on his mind out in the open.

"Things have been different for me lately, and I haven't known what to think about it. My father always says the best approach is the straightforward approach, just to be honest and open. You are an amazing person Rita, beautiful and smart and talented. I have fought it for the longest time, but it has finally beaten me down. I am in love with you, Rita, and I need to find out if you could ever think about me that way too." Paul turned to look at Rita, not daring to move a muscle or blink for fear that he would miss something that might give him a clue about what she was thinking.

Rita sat there on the wall next to Paul, in shock, never expecting to hear what he had just said to her. She could have more easily accepted a declaration that he was a visitor from another planet, like a movie that they had seen recently, as to hear him say that he was in love with her. She couldn't get her head wrapped around the idea; it just wasn't making any sense to her. She sat there dumbfounded, looking back at him blankly, having no idea what she might say in return. Such a thing had never even occurred to her, and the young man sitting next to her, she still saw as the brother he had always been.

Paul mistook Rita's silence for relief, because she was feeling the same thing that she was feeling. It gave him the courage to lean forward and venture a tentative kiss on Rita's lips.

For an instant Rita sat there motionless, as if she had turned to stone and had become a part of the wall she was sitting on. When the reality of it finally reached her, she jerked away from him and stood up to go.

"I'm sorry Rita, please don't go. I had to tell you, it just wouldn't stay inside my heart any more, it felt like I was drowning." Paul hung his head, in shame and embarrassment, not able to look Rita in the eyes.

Rita felt a wave of compassion for her oldest and dearest friend. This must have been terrible for him, and she tried to soften the blow. "Paul, there is no one on this earth that is closer to me, or knows me better than you do. I love you with all of my heart, but it is the love of a sister for a brother. I can't even imagine you being in love with me, much less me being in love with you. I don't know what to say to make this any easier for you, but I will do anything I can to help you work through this." Rita smiled, and gave Paul a hug, like she had given him a thousand times before. She hoped he understood, and would still be her brother.

Paul nodded sadly, trying to put on a brave face, as they mounted up and headed in the direction of the Castle. When they reached the stable they unsaddled the horses, rubbed them down, and fed and watered them. They tried to make small talk, but there was a big barrier separating them, and they both felt it. Paul, for his part, was angry with himself for making Rita feel uncomfortable with his company. Rita was sad for the feelings she couldn't return for Paul, and felt awkward about his declaration of love and the kiss. At this moment, they both felt like strangers for the first time in their lives.

Donna Lucia and Nina were cutting some flowers for the table when they came in, and noticed they weren't their usually talkative selves. They just headed off in different directions to get changed out of their riding clothes, because it was almost time for dinner. Even though Guido and Beppe were dirty and tired from their work in the garden, they had their usual game of cards on the patio with a good glass of Grappa.

Anna had waited for Rita to return, and became concerned; she was not usually this late getting back. When she returned, Rita didn't say much about her ride like she usually did, and just headed up to her room to change. Anna picked up on her daughter's unusual mood right away, but decided Rita would talk about what was bothering her when she was ready.

Beppe and Guido looked up at Paul's approach, and noticed they didn't get his normal cheery greeting. "Are you all right Paul?" asked Beppe, turning to watch his son climbing up the steps towards the back of the Castle.

"Sure Papa, Uncle Guido, everything's fine" Paul tried to lighten his mood and waved to reassure Beppe and Guido. "I am just a little tired and hot and dirty from my ride. I won't be long." With that he beat a hasty retreat before these two men who knew him so well could ask him any more questions. He had no intentions of talking about what was bothering him. Beppe and Guido just looked at each other, wondering what could have put Paul in such an uncharacteristically glum frame of mind.

Guido had an uneasy feeling as he watched his nephew walk away, so he threw in his cards and got to his feet. "I'd better go see if the women are almost ready, it isn't like them to be late." With that Guido picked up his crutches and headed off in the direction of the chalet.

Beppe, sensing the worry in his brother, called after him, "Hurry back, I want to open a new bottle of wine tonight."

Anna found an excuse to go into Rita's room, carrying a load of fresh laundry that needed to be put away. She had her back to Rita as she put clothes in the dresser, but she was listening for any opening to get Rita talking. "So, how was your ride, it seemed like such a nice day today."

Rita didn't say anything for a moment. She needed to talk, but she didn't want to talk either. It was confusing, and she couldn't decide which way to go with the feelings crashing around inside her head. Finally she decided to confide in the woman she loved like a mother, and sat down on her bed with a thump. "Paul seemed troubled while we were out riding this afternoon, so I tried to get him to talk to me. I thought he might be worried about something at school, or some of the things we saw on the newsreels that they show before the movie at the theater. What he said took me totally by surprise." Rita paused, looking over at Anna, before she dropped a bomb shell on her that was going to change her life, as it had Rita's.

"What did he say?" asked Anna, casually keeping a neutral face, but thinking at a hundred miles per hour.

"He said he was in love with me, and then he kissed me," replied Rita in a rush, getting it out before she lost her nerve.

Anna was speechless, looking back at Rita with the half-full laundry basket still in her arms. "What did you do?" she finally thought to ask, stalling for time to get a grip on what she had just heard.

"I was shocked, and pulled away. I could tell it hurt Paul's feelings, so I tried to let him down easy. I told him I loved him with all of my heart, but it was the love of a sister for a brother. He took it very well, but I could tell it embarrassed him, and hurt his pride. We didn't say much as we rode back, and took care of the horses. I feel just awful for him, but he has always been my brother, how else am I supposed to feel?" finished Rita, as if a huge weight had been lifted off of her chest and she could breathe again.

The sound of the front door opening up reached Rita's room, and Guido hollered up "Hey, are you girls almost ready? Dinner will be served soon, and Beppe is opening a bottle of the new wine tonight to see how the vintage is shaping up. With the rains we had last year, it should be a very good year." Guido, kept talking, trying to figure out what was going on upstairs, where he couldn't go.

"Yes, my dear," called Anna, in a cheery tone she didn't feel. "You go ahead. Rita is still getting changed, and we will be over shortly."

Guido knew his wife well enough to tell something was up; but he wasn't going to get any answers standing here. He had a mystery to solve, and the walk over to the Castle on his crutches gave him time to think and consider.

Beppe was watching out the window for Guido, and was relieved when he saw him coming. "Well, it's about time you got back" joked Beppe, "I thought I was going to have to drink this bottle of wine all by myself. Where are the ladies?"

"Oh, you know how women are," laughed Guido, "It takes them longer to get ready than us. They are much prettier and have much more hair to comb!" The two friends who didn't have as much hair as they used to, had a good laugh, and Beppe poured some wine in the glasses to ease the tension he could feel in the room.

"Let's drink to this good wine! It was a good harvest, and a very good vintage. It will do well when we send it to market" added Guido, with another appreciative sip from his glass.

Donna Lucia and Paul showed up about the same time, taking their place at the table, and picking up their own wine glasses. "This is wonderful" confirmed Donna Lucia. "This is the best wine we have produced since the war ended. It has really made a big difference now that we have enough good people to properly prune and tie up the vines."

Paul sat there quietly, sipping his wine, and swirling it around in his glass, as if he were considering the color of it. His silence made Beppe and Guido even more concerned, and wondered what could be the reason for his low spirits.

Finally Anna and Rita entered the dining room with a flourish, and took their seats. Anna sat next to Guido, and took his hand as she always did. He felt her hand was unusually cold and he rubbed it between his own hands to warm it up. Rita was calm and serene as she took her seat next to Paul, but she didn't look at him, or speak to him as was her habit. Anna squeezed Guido's hand, but didn't say anything.

Beppe and Donna Lucia were mystified, looking at Paul and Rita. They were both sitting like polite strangers, neither saying a word. The silence in the dining room seemed like a cloud that threatens to rain at any minute.

Rita finally broke the silence, as she addressed her extended family. "Paul and I had a nice ride today, but I could tell something was bothering him. We stopped and sat on the old stone wall in the upper meadow, so we could have an opportunity to talk. He told me he has had different feelings for me lately, but he didn't know what to do about them. Uncle Beppe, you have always told us the best way to approach any problem it to be straightforward and honest." Paul, was looking down at his plate, as he was waiting for the revelation that was about to come forth. He felt comforted by the sound of Rita's familiar voice, and he was grateful that she would be the one to tell their family, she had always had a better way with words than he did.

Rita straightened her shoulders, and went head first into her tale, one that might change her family forever. "Paul told me he loved me, and wanted to know if I could ever feel that way for him in return. I couldn't have been more surprised if he had sprouted wings and flew off over the trees. He must have taken my silence for approval, so he kissed me. I pulled away from him, and I could see he was hurt by my actions. I tried to tell him as gently as I could that I didn't feel that way about him. I love Paul, with all of my heart, and I love all of you here at this table tonight. Paul is my brother, and I love him like my brother. Anything else would just feel awkward and wrong to me."

Everyone was stunned at the tale they had just heard, never considering that something like this might ever arise. They all looked at each other, at a loss of words, not knowing what to think.

"I am concerned that I have hurt Paul to the core of his soul, and it will be difficult for him to be around me in the future. Things have certainly changed between us, and I don't want anyone here to feel uncomfortable because of this. I was thinking that perhaps I should move back to my father's old apartment in town. It might be easier for everyone here if I was gone for a while, to let everything settle down, and we can see the way ahead for the future of our family." Rita turned and looked at Paul for the first time since she sat down, hoping desperately that her brother was still in there somewhere, and that he could find it in his heart to forgive her.

Beppe was the first to find his voice, and he screamed out "No! No!" He stood up so fast that his chair fell over backwards on the floor behind him. "Whatever else has happened, we are a family! Families come together in difficult situations, and support each other. I can't bear the thought of you sitting in that little apartment of Guido's in town all alone, with no one to be there for you but Grandma Delia. We are a family, a strong family. We have gone through a war together, faced hard times, and shared our grief when those we loved have passed beyond our embrace. We will face this too, and we will find a solution so that we can look into each other's eyes and laugh again, and enjoy each other's company! We will be as we have always been: people who love each other, unconditionally, no matter what."

Donna Lucia had never heard her husband speak so passionately, and reached up to squeeze his hand. He looked down at her, and saw the tears of pride and support standing in her eyes. He looked over at Guido, and his brother stared back at him, with the same expression that was reflected in Donna Lucia's eyes. Anna smiled back at the people she loved most in the world, and felt the strength of their bonds.

Paul had been listening to every word spoken by those he loved, and finally rose to his own feet to speak. "I am so grateful to be blessed to be a member of this great family. It has been very difficult to deal with all of the things occurring in my life just now, both personally and as a member of our community. First of all, Rita, I owe you a profound apology. When we talked this afternoon, I was only focusing on my own thoughts and needs. I didn't stop to think what it would be like for you, if you didn't share my feelings. I have no excuse, I was wrong to put that off on you, when I could have opted to be patient and observant instead. If I had done that, I would have clearly seen the answer to the question that was so important to me, without making you feel ill at ease in my company. I would like to concur with what my father has said, we are a strong family, and we will work this out. We are stronger together, than we are apart. I would never forgive myself if you moved into town, Rita, to ease the discomfort I have caused by my selfish and ill considered actions.

I have been thinking for some time about what I want to do about my education. I had planned on beginning my training here, as a doctor, at the hospital in Lake Braies because it was local and they have a very highly respected teaching curriculum. However, one of the finest facilities, in this part of the world, is in Geneva, Switzerland, not really all that far away. We have family that lives nearby, and I could live with them, and attend the University at Geneva. Italy has become a very troubled place; with the rise of Fascism eclipsing all that I have been raised to believe in. I do not want to get caught up in that snare, and be forced to support their perverse ideals. With your permission, father and mother, I would like to send in my application to the medical school there in Geneva, and begin my studies next semester."

Beppe looked at his wife for a long moment, and then looked at the rest of the family gathered around the table. He also looked at all of the servants standing quietly around the edges of the room, still holding the bowls and trays of the dinner that was now cold. These people were also members of this large extended family, and they were listening to every word, weighing each and every syllable in their own hearts.

Guido was the one who found his feet and his voice first. "Paul, we are all struggling with the things we have heard this evening, and your father is right, we are a strong family and we will get through this together. We don't want you to leave, in the midst of such uncertain times. Perhaps Anna and Rita and I could move back into town, for a little while, until we have all had time to come to terms with these monumental changes. We couldn't have loved you more as a son, if you had been born to us. God has blessed us with the privilege of being part of your life and helping you grow to manhood." Guido had tears standing in his eyes, with the clear affection he felt for Paul, and the pain he felt for Paul and Rita's anguish.

"That won't be necessary, Papa," began Rita, slowly rising to her own feet, and turning to face Paul. "I have always believed you could love someone, and not like them. I have always loved you Paul, we are best friends, and you are dearer to me than my own life. When I think of all of the unhappy people I have seen over the years, who are married, but don't like each other, I think that is the epitome of sadness. I can think of worse things in the world, than to be married to your best friend. I may never be able to love you the way that you love me, but I do love you and respect you. If you will have me," paused Rita, carefully considering her next words, "I will marry you."

Paul looked into Rita's eyes, staring back at him with open honesty and sincerity. He wasn't worthy to stand in the same room with this most noble of all women, much less stand next to her in the Chapel. He slowly reached out his arms to her, and she came to him willingly, without a moment's hesitation or reservation. "I can't tell you what this means to me," Paul whispered into her hair, bathing it with his tears. "But, I can't allow you to sacrifice yourself like that. I will go to Geneva and concentrate on my studies. When I have graduated, if Italy is still here and in one piece, I will return home. We will see how we feel about each other then. I have heard that absence makes the heart grow fonder, let us put that theory to the test and leave the future to itself."

"I am proud of you, my son," Beppe said. "We will, of course, support your decision to seek your training in Geneva. Well! What did I tell you? We are a strong family, and we will always prevail. Now, why don't we get the food heated back up and have our dinner! There is enough good wine on the table, and enough good conversation to see us through until dinner is served." Beppe smiled at the servants, who had been as still as the statutes they were standing next to. They all smiled back at him, and hurried off to the kitchen to reheat the food, and get it back on the table.

The next few days were a flurry of activity, as everyone rushed to help Paul put together all of the things he would need while he was away at school. He immediately sent off his application to Geneva, with a number of strong endorsements from teachers and longtime family friends who worked and taught at the hospital in Lake Braies. Everyone was confident that Paul, with his outstanding records and the strength of his recommendations would be accepted easily. Rita spent as much time with Paul as she could in those final busy days, glad that they had found a way around the wall that had so unexpectedly appeared between them. They both felt the cloud that had hovered over the lifelong bonds they had developed; vanish in the dawn of understanding and patience and respect.

The last dinner they enjoyed together was an occasion for both celebrating and sadness. Paul looked around at his family and friends, scarcely able to believe that this was the last time he would see any of them for the next four years. To be sure, he would be very busy; he knew that by observing the young Interns at the hospital. They were constantly hurrying to keep up, and always in a rush to be somewhere else. They struggled to find a balance between their studies, and the demands of their practical experience. The constant forays with established doctors making the rounds of the hospital corridors, made sleeping and eating rare luxuries. Still, he was sure that there would be those moments that would threaten to overwhelm him, as he thought about all that he was leaving behind.

His father and mother kept looking at him, as if they were trying to permanently etch him in their minds and their hearts. Guido and Anna looked like they wanted to rush over, hug him, and never let him go. The servants would find a way of conveying their feelings by leaving a little extra on his plate, or an unexpected treat that he loved.

Rita was the most amazing of all. The new dress she bought for this special occasion was absolutely beautiful, but paled in comparison to the radiance of her smile. To think he almost ruined that expression he might never see in her eyes again, Paul thought, after his incredible blunder on their ride. He was grateful for a second chance, and with time, he might yet see a different expression in Rita's eyes. After all, look at Anna and Guido. Anna was content with her life when she came to live at the Castle, and let Guido know in no uncertain terms that she intended for it to stay that way! The only thing that was certain in life was change. He would focus on that, and let the future continue to unfold as it had a mind to.

After dinner, Paul and Rita took a final walk in the gardens that they had grown up in and loved so well. The moon was just coming up over the edge of the trees by the lake. The "Man in the Moon" was smiling down on them, as if to say that everything would work out for the best. The roses were in full bloom, and their fragrance filled the air as they strolled along the paths, companionably holding each other's hand. They talked and laughed, and remembered things from their childhood. Rolling up their pant legs and catching polliwogs in the shallows, never having a prayer to catch the smarter and faster frogs. Sitting on the limb of a tree, and watching the baby birds as they slowly pecked their way out of the speckled shells in the spring. There was the time they were digging with Guido, preparing a new area to plant another flower garden. They discovered a Roman statue in the soil that must have been left behind by another gardener, and forgotten hundreds of years before. It was a magical evening, and you could almost see a Fairy Queen and her entire court dancing on the moon lit meadow, with the crickets and the frogs providing the music for their grand ball.

They finally stopped and sat in the gazebo, to look at the lake and watch the moon sailing majestically on its smooth unbroken surface. Perhaps it was the idyllic setting that would have been the envy of any romance novelist. Perhaps it was the fact that this would be the last time they would see each other for a long time, and the world was steadily becoming a more uncertain place. Perhaps it was that they had always been close, since before they could remember. Whatever the reason, either individually, or acting in concert, their mood slowly began to change. A kiss in a meadow, that just days ago had seemed hurried and clumsy, was now easy and natural. The barriers of friendship now seemed to expand and grow, as they sat there in the glow of the moon. What passed between them was for them alone, and something they would both examine again and again in the years that would separate them. The faint rays of a newborn sun as it lit the morning sky, was finally the herald that bid the two of them farewell, as they made their way home separately.

Anna kept her lone vigil in the front room, manning her station at the window, as Rita opened the front door. Guido had long since gone to bed; content to let the two of them say their goodbyes, on their own terms. Perhaps he was thinking of a tearful farewell in a railroad station a lifetime ago. Rita, when she saw her mother, smiled, and came closer to give her a hug, and rest her head on Anna's shoulder. Anna had no words for the daughter that fate had blessed her with. They just stood there together, each alone in her own thoughts, with memories of all of the firsts in their life. No words were necessary between the two women, one who had long since bid her youth good bye, and the other who was just now realizing all of the possibilities before her.

Chapter Eleven

Paul rode to the station in the car with Beppe, Donna Lucia, Guido, Anna, and Rita. It was a quiet ride, as they watched the trees pass by, and the cows raised their heads to look at the car. Earlier that morning, a good many of the staff had helped to load Paul's baggage on the big horse-drawn wagon, and had taken it down to the loading platform to await the train. Deciding it would be too much work for the aging baggage handler, they all stayed on to help with the loading. Getting to say one last goodbye to Paul was just a happy consequence of their kind and generous natures.

Paul stood there, hugging each and every member in his family. Surprisingly, the male members of his household required just as many handkerchiefs to wipe their eyes as the female members. It would seem that there must be a lot of extra pollen in the air this morning, and those standing nearest the approaching train were feeling the effects most acutely.

Their final words were lost, as the great engine applied its steam brakes, and the train paused to let off passengers who had reached their destination, and take on those who were just starting their travels. The goodbyes all around them were the same. There were hugs and tears and baskets of sandwiches for the trip. Promises of calls and letters, and a last farewell as the train slowly gained speed, heading off to its next destination. Paul and Rita had already said their goodbyes last night, and they settled for a prolonged wave, continuing until the train was out of sight.

The ride to Switzerland was a good time for Paul to think, and to mentally shift gears for the next chapter in his life. The breathtaking mountains, and sparkling rivers, and endless meadows had the familiar feel of home, though they were farther away with every mile that passed.

Chapter Twelve

It had been quite some time since Paul had seen his Aunt and Uncle. To the world they were His Highness Duke Emil Von Strass, and Her Highness Duchess Rosemary Von Strass. His cousin, Count Philip Von Strass, was almost his age, and they would be attending the University together. Philip was also interested in medicine, so Paul would not be a total stranger in a strange place. He would have someone to make introductions for him, and help him as a study partner. They would live in the Palace, for the first few months while the two of them got their bearings. As their studies and labs began to take up an ever increasing amount of their waking hours, it was decided that the hour it took them to get to class could be better spent elsewhere. Paul and Philip moved into the dormitories together, and the two cousins made the transition to university life easily.

Switzerland was able to declare its neutrality, and remain for the most part untouched by the storms that were sweeping over the rest of Europe. The insatiable hunger of Hitler for domination of every country that came under his greedy gaze was feed by his Blitzkrieg strategy. His Panzer divisions rolled over all that opposed them, only slowing to refuel their machines of war. Mussolini dragged Italy along on this ride with the Valkeries, burying everything that was good and noble in the soul of the Italian people. There were hushed whispers of unfortunate groups of people who had attracted the animosity of those in power. Jews and Gypsies and political dissidents were rounded up and sent away. Few people knew where they went, and were afraid to ask about their fate. It was a time to keep what you thought to yourself, and concentrate on trying to keep your family alive, and avoid bringing attention to yourself.

Lake Braies felt like it was a world away from all that filled the papers and news reels in the theater. In the fall of 1942, Beppe and Guido were still doing their best to care for the Castle and the Estate. A number of the younger men had already been drafted, to swell the ranks of Mussolini's black shirted army. It was inevitable that the trouble would eventually spill over their beautiful mountains, which had always been so important strategically to every army that had ever marched.

Beppe and Guido were enjoying the last of a warm autumn day, walking and discussing all of the craziness that was overtaking Europe. No matter how they looked at the things they had learned about, it didn't make any sense to them. Germany had been their enemy, when they had fought in the last World War and now somehow they had become allies! It was hard for the two of them to ever consider a German as a friend; they had lost too many of their Alpini brothers to the scourge that was Germany and Austria.

In their favorite sitting room in the Castle, Donna Lucia, Anna, and Nina were enjoying a pleasant afternoon together, working on their various projects. Anna and Nina were working on a quilt together, and Lucia was crocheting a blanket to send to Paul in Switzerland. While Beppe and Guido were outside near the great fountain by the entrance, a shiny black Mercedes sedan turned into the long gravel driveway. There was something about it that made them both uncomfortable, as if the car were a harbinger of bad tidings. The big car lumbered to a stop by the front entrance, and a former Bersagliere of the First World War emerged from its roomy interior. It was a man known to many in the Alpini, a brave hero of Italy. Sergeant Neri was now dressed in the black shirt of the Fascists, and it was hard to see this once honorable man wearing the livery of those who would destroy their beloved homeland.

Behind Sergeant Neri, a German officer appeared from the dark interior of the car, and the driver clicked his heels in the traditional military salute. A second German soldier remained in the car, apparently waiting for orders from his superior.

"Good evening to you, Captain Beppe Donat" called out Sergeant Neri. "It is good to see you so well and fit. I am delighted to see you as well Sergeant Guido Marron!

Even on crutches you are still a better soldier than any for miles around."

"Well, Sergeant Neri," replied Guido in return, "I can't say you look too well these days, the pallor of your skin doesn't look too healthy. Perhaps it is that black shirt you are wearing; I believe you looked better in the green of the Alpini. I hope you haven't come all the way out here to arrest us!"

Beppe was watching the German officer that was standing next to the Mercedes, listening quietly to the exchange going on between the two Alpini. It was clear that he understood Italian and was following the conversation closely. He didn't seem to react to the decidedly unfriendly tone towards his country. He finally stepped away from the car, and came to stand by Sergeant Neri.

Neri, for his part didn't seem to notice the officer, as he continued his conversation with Guido. "Arrest you?!" cried Neri, with shock and amazement clearly displayed on his face. "What an idea! You are among the most respected heroes of Italy. It would be insanity to arrest you. I might just as well go home and shoot myself; I would never betray my comrades in such a cowardly manner! I am here to introduce you to this gentleman next to me. He is a German Captain, but his rank is of no importance to him. He is a world class doctor, and has come to Lake Braies because he has heard of our fine hospital, and he wants to help us improve it and make it into an even better facility. Captain Donat, and Sergeant Marron, please allow me to introduce Dr. Kruger."

In flawless Italian, the German officer spoke to Beppe and Guido, "It is a pleasure to finally get to meet the two of you; I have heard so many complimentary things about you from Sergeant Neri. You have a beautiful home, and your town reminds me of my own small town back in Germany. I have come to inspect your fine hospital, and see what I can do to improve and expand it. Your location is perfect for the needs of wounded soldiers, and it is an unfortunate fact of war that where there is fighting, there will be wounded soldiers. It is my hope that I can expand the current capabilities of the hospital, by adding services that are not currently available here." With that Dr. Kruger, bowed his head as a sign of respect to Beppe and Guido, and clicked the heels of his shiny boots together smartly, but he did not raise his arm in salute and add "Heil Hitler."

Neither of the men was prepared to soften their view of the German, just because he spoke Italian. We are pleased to hear that you have come to help our hospital, Captain Kruger. As you have pointed out it is a fine facility, but there are a number of specialties currently not available. People from our region have to travel to the hospital in Trento, when they need such services. It will be good if they can receive treatment here, instead of traveling so far." Beppe used the German's military title on purpose, not ready to accept him on the word of a man who was clearly in the employ of the Fascists.

"That is our intention; it will be a great benefit to the entire region to have another full service hospital available. It is my hope that while I am here working at the hospital I will be able to get to know both of you better. Sergeant Neri has commented on the quality of the wine you produce here, he says it is among the finest in Italy. Perhaps we can have a glass of it, to judge the veracity of his boast." Kruger smiled back at Beppe and Guido, trying to ease the tension that was still floating in their polite words.

"I hope you have not come to requisition our good Grappa, the demands of the government for additional supplies for their army have already been acutely felt in our markets." Guido answered, with as much sarcasm as he dared with the German Officer.

"Again you misunderstand my intentions, I was only hoping for a sample of your wine. My own home town produces an excellent wine, and I find what I have had available to me since I left home has been very poor in comparison." Dr. Kruger smiled again, hoping to find some common ground to begin a relationship with two of the key citizens of Lake Braies.

"Of course, where are my manners? It is selfish of me to deny you the pleasure of sampling our wine," intoned Beppe, thinking to learn a little more about this German doctor, and the true reason for his appearance in Lake Braies. "It is a nice afternoon; perhaps you and

Sergeant Neri would like to join us on the veranda for a glass of wine."

"Thank you, Count Donat, that is very kind of you," replied Kruger. "We have a fairly demanding schedule, but I think there should always be time for a good glass of Grappa."

This obviously pleased both Beppe and Guido, as they had a similar sentiment. No matter how busy they were, they found time in their hectic day to enjoy a bottle of Grappa and a pleasant conversation with a game of cards. They led the way to the back of the Castle, and Beppe sent word ahead to bring glasses and a bottle of their new vintage to the patio. Beppe opened the bottle of wine, and poured out a good quantity in each of the glasses. There were also several plates of snacks that would go well with the wine, and show it off to its best advantage.

The German held up his wine glass, and sniffed the glass, appreciating the aroma of the Grappa. He held his glass up to the light, examining the color as he swirled the ruby liquid. Beppe and Guido were pleased that he seemed to understand how to appreciate fine wine, instead of just guzzling it down like a barbarian drinking swill. He finally tasted it, with his eyes closed, obviously savoring the flavor of the wine as he held it in his mouth. When he opened his eyes, the look on his face was of a man who had finally been given something wonderful to enjoy, after a very long drought.

"I can see that I am going to have to be careful when I listen to Sergeant Neri's opinions in the future, his estimation of this wine was woefully understated. If I had not seen you pour the wine out of the bottle and into the glasses with my own eyes, I would think that you had given me a wine from my own town to play a trick on me. This is absolutely wonderful, and very much appreciated next to the beverages I have had to endure. I say beverages because they are liquid, and you can swallow them, but they hardly qualify as wine!" Kruger smiled with a sincere expression on his face.

"It is very good of you to offer such high praise for our grappa. It has been a tough job to bring the vines back up to their former quality since the last war. Now I hope we will not lose ground again because of the new troubles that once again darken our horizons." Beppe looked at the doctor, with a pointed look that said he hoped the Germans had not brought them any new challenges to afflict their lives.

"That is something we all hope for" replied Kruger honestly. "I understand that you have a son who is also going to be a doctor, Count Donat. He is currently attending the University in Geneva and is doing well in his studies there. That will be a real asset to the hospital here; Geneva is one of the top medical schools in the world. I also heard that you have a daughter that is interested in medicine as well, Mr. Marron. She is currently enrolled in the nurse's training classes here at the hospital in Lake Braies. You must both be so proud of your children, preparing to be of service to their community with such important skills."

"You seem to be well informed on the lives of our citizens here in Lake Braies," began Guido. "It is a shame that you are not as insightful into other more pressing matters. Mussolini is leading Italy down a road to disaster, with the ideals he holds dear. Germany is overreaching its own boarders in a similar quest for domination. The problem with reaching too far is you can slip and fall." Guido paused and looked down at his empty pant leg. "When will you learn a lesson that has been taught over and over again?"

The German didn't change the expression on his face, as he sat and gave Guido his full attention. He didn't appear to take offense at Guido's frank words. "You are very wise, it does seem that we commit the same mistakes over and over again, don't we? Unfortunately it is not something that I can do anything about, that is far above my pay grade. I do what I can on a personal level, helping to care for those given into my charge as a doctor. I try to improve conditions where I can, and leave the rest to God."

"I can understand the doctor's position; he can't help it if he was born a German. But you, Sergeant Neri, you know better. You fought to protect Italy, in the last war, the same as we did. How can a good Alpini stoop to help this Fascist plague?" Guido was clearly outraged at the betrayal of one of his own, and was warming up to his subject.

"I have learned to go where the wind blows, and you would do well to think about that carefully," spat back Neri, irritated by Guido's attitude.

"That is the danger with a cold wind, if you are not careful, you can catch pneumonia." Guido fired back, unwilling to back down to Neri, even with the German clearly following the heated exchange between the two former comrades in arms.

That comment made the German laugh out loud, startling everyone sitting at the table. Beppe looked at the doctor, and was amazed at the genuine amusement on his face. Perhaps there was more to this man than the uniform and shiny boots he was wearing. Beppe decided to give him the benefit of the doubt and have a better look. It is said that you should keep your friends close, and your enemies closer. It was probably prudent to get to know this German doctor better, so Beppe decided to try the diplomatic approach.

"It is getting late," injected Beppe into the uncomfortable silence, as Guido and Neri glared at each other. "We still have a number of things to attend to, and the sun is not a patient or understanding task master. Dr Kruger, would you like to dine with us tomorrow evening? It would give you an opportunity to meet the ladies of our household, and give us a better chance to exchange ideas about the hospital. I am sorry we won't be able to entertain you in the style we might have in happier times. Our pantry and larder is somewhat depleted since we have had to provide more supplies for the army. It may be simpler fare, but our wines will more than make up for the modest meal." Guido looked at Beppe in surprise, never imaging that he would invite the German into the Castle. He knew Beppe well enough to trust that he had a good reason for the invitation, and didn't show any reaction. A dinner might be a more relaxed venue to speak with the German, and get a better feel for his true intentions.

"I am honored by your gracious invitation, Count Donat. I myself grew up in a very humble family, and I am the first one ever to get a college education. I never dreamed, as I was growing up, that I would be invited to attend a meal with such a noble family as yours. I will look forward with great anticipation to meeting your fine ladies. If they are anything like you and Mr. Marron, I am sure they will be a delight to visit with." He and Sergeant Neri rose to leave, and after a cordial farewell, headed in the direction of the black Mercedes. The doctor paused to speak to the uniformed driver, and the driver made some notes in his book. He then came to attention and saluted, before he closed the door for Dr. Kruger, and went around to the other side of the car and got in. The car started up immediately, and slowly made its way down the gravel driveway.

Beppe looked at Guido, knowing what he wanted to talk about. "My dear friend, these are troubled times. It is a good idea to find out all you can about your enemy, so you can be prepared to deal with him. Even an enemy can be a useful tool in times of want and shortages. Let us see what he has to say, without the company of Sergeant Neri. Our good Grappa will be a very effective lubricant to ease his tongue, and help us to learn what kind of a man the German doctor really is." Beppe looked at Guido, hoping he could count on his brother's agreement and support for his plan. Perhaps Guido would be more even tempered in his conduct with the company of the women.

"You are very wise, my friend. I shouldn't have run off at the mouth like I did with Neri. It made me so mad to see him aiding the enemies of Italy. His black shirt was a slap in the face to every one of our brothers who gave their lives protecting our homes and our freedom. It won't happen again. If he really is here to help improve our hospital, I don't guess it matters what uniform he is wearing. What do you say we go tell Lucia and Anna and Rita that we are going to have guests tomorrow evening? Women don't like last minute surprises, they can be more dangerous that the worst enemy cannons!" The two brothers laughed at Guido's insightful observation. It would take some careful planning to put a presentable meal on the table.

Early the next morning the black Mercedes made an unexpected visit to the Castle. This time there were only the two German soldiers in the car, as it came to rest in front of the entrance to the Castle. The passenger got out, and climbed the steps, and knocked politely at the huge front door. Beppe opened the door and was surprised to see the German Sergeant standing there.

"Good morning Count Donat" began the soldier politely, clearly aware that he was speaking to a man due honor and respect. "I was ordered to deliver some supplies to you for your dinner party this evening. They come with Dr. Kruger's compliments and he said to tell you he is looking forward with anticipation to the evening. He will arrive at 7:30, if that will be convenient." The Sergeant waited patiently for Beppe to reply, and give instructions on where he would like the supplies unloaded.

"That was very thoughtful of the Doctor; please convey our thanks to him for his gracious gift. We will look forward to seeing him at 7:30. If you will drive around to the back of the building, I will have someone there to help you unload." Beppe told the Sergeant. With that the German also clicked his heels together in a loud snap, but did not raise his arm in salute either.

Guido was standing beside Beppe at the front door, watching the German make his way back down the stairs to the car. "See, I told you it was a good idea to be polite to your enemy!" laughed Beppe.

"It is little more than charity, throwing us a few crumbs. It is nothing in comparison to what they have taken from us," grumbled Guido in complaint. "Still, it is a polite and respectful gesture on the part of the Doctor. I will admit, in spite of my better judgment, I am starting to like him."

"That's good," complimented Beppe, giving Guido a hug. "Things can change rapidly in life, and it is far better to keep a positive outlook. We can miss opportunities if we are only looking for the bad in people. I have heard it said "If you look for the good in people, you will surely find it," and I have found that is true. Let's go see if there is anything we can do to help with dinner."

Chapter Thirteen

At the appointed time, the black Mercedes pulled up to the front door. Beppe and Guido were surprised to see that the Doctor was accompanied by a military escort. They made no attempt to enter with the doctor; they just stationed themselves outside, clearly waiting for the doctor to finish his visit. The doctor was not dressed in his uniform, but was wearing a nice charcoal gray double breasted suit for the occasion. He was also carrying a large bouquet of flowers for the ladies of the Castle.

"Good evening Count Donat and Mr. Marron, I trust I have not kept you waiting?" Dr. Kruger bowed slightly in greeting.

"Not at all, you are right on time. May I present my wife, Countess Donna Lucia?" Beppe held out his hand to his wife, and she stepped forward to meet the doctor.

"I am very honored to meet you, your Highness," the doctor answered, reaching out to take Lucia's hand, and kissing it in a very formal greeting.

"Welcome to our home, Dr. Kruger" responded Donna Lucia, every bit the noble woman she was born to be.

Beppe spoke again, finishing the introductions, "This is Mrs. Anna Marron."

Dr. Kruger turned to address Anna, in exactly the same manner that he had greeted Lucia. He clearly thought of her as an equal in station to the Countess he had just addressed, and it impressed Beppe. They had never recognized titles or formalities here in the Castle, but he was pleased that the doctor had shown the same deference to Anna as he had to Donna Lucia.

"I am disappointed that Mr. Marron is not here, will he be joining us later?" the doctor asked, noting Guido's absence.

"His leg is giving him some problems today, and it has slowed him down. I am sure he will be here as soon as he can. He can be a very stubborn man, and he refuses to go see the doctor about the pain he has been experiencing lately. The prosthetic leg is a help to him, but it can make him sore as well. I would be grateful if you would offer to look at it when he arrives. He doesn't like to make the trip into the town for something he considers so minor, but perhaps he would allow you to look at it since you are a doctor, and you are already here."

"I would be happy to; I know the story of how he lost his leg. It is a good idea to have it checked periodically. There is nothing wrong with being stubborn, it is the mark of a man who can get things accomplished, when other men might quit. I noticed there was something wrong when I was here yesterday. His leg seemed to be causing him pain every time he moved.

Perhaps I can employ the persuasive power of the ladies to prevail upon Mr. Marron to allow me to examine his leg." The doctor seemed sincere in his interest to help Guido, and Beppe didn't intend to let this opportunity for expert medical attention to pass because of Guido's pride.

At that moment, the front door opened, and Guido made his way slowly inside on his crutches. Beppe whispered to the doctor, "Speaking of the devil..."

"Good evening, Captain Doctor Kruger," greeted Guido, slightly out of breath from the exertion of walking over from the chalet. "You look like a real gentleman dressed like that; it suits you better than your uniform." The doctor nodded at Guido's attempt to compliment him, but his mind was on the task of getting this proud man to show him his leg.

"Thank you, this is my favorite suit. Alpino Sergeant Guido Marron, I know you do not like me, and in truth, I don't care for you very much either. That is of no importance, since I am a doctor, a very good doctor. When you become a doctor, you take the same oath as every other physician, no matter where you are from. I promised to help those who needed me, and I can see you are in pain. I ask you to look beyond our differences, and help me to keep the oath I made when I became a doctor, by allowing me to examine your leg."

Everyone in the room held their breath, not expecting the doctor to be so abrupt and forthright with Guido. They couldn't even guess how Guido would take this request, even from someone he trusted and liked.

When Guido's reaction did come, it was not what they expected at all!

Guido stared at the man standing there in the foyer, and didn't move for a moment. Then he threw back his head and let go with a peel of laughter that none of them had heard from Guido in a good long while. When Guido finally got control of himself, he wiped his eyes on his shirt, to clear the tears.

"I like the direct approach," continued Guido, still chuckling at the audacity of the German's words. "No beating around the bush, you just come right out and say what is on your mind. I can respect that, because I am a man who speaks my mind as well." With that, Guido made his way over to a chair, and rolled up his pant leg for the doctor to examine him.

After a brief look, Dr. Kruger nodded and said, "I thought as well. I will need some clean sponges and plenty of hot water. Is there someplace more convenient where I can take care of this leg?"

"Of course" said Beppe, indicating the way to the study. "There is much better light in here, and we will get you anything that you need."

"My dear Alpino, I can't do anything about your stubborn nature, you would make a mule look like an obedient dog. I can, however treat your leg, and make you much more comfortable, on one condition." The doctor said, grinning at Guido.

"What can I do to help you, doctor?" Guido looked back, clearly mystified at what he could possibly do to assist the doctor.

"It would be a great help if you didn't talk so much!" the German said, trying to keep a straight face. With that everyone in the room laughed, clearly relieved by the doctor's humor, and the easing of the tension in the air. While they were still laughing, the doctor pulled a small notebook out of his pocket and wrote a short note. He walked over to the front door, opened it, and handed the note to the guard standing there. He saluted smartly, and turned to take care of his assignment.

At that moment, Beppe emerged from the dining room, carrying a new bottle of wine, and some glasses. "Perhaps we can have a little good grappa anesthetic, to help ease your leg, my friend, and help your doctor overlook your shortcomings."

The front door opened again, and Rita walked in, clearly confused by what she was seeing. Her father was sitting on a comfortable chair in the study with his pant leg rolled back, and the leg looked red and swollen.

"What is going on here?" said Rita, eyeing the strange man standing with her family.

Guido was the one who spoke up this time. "I am sorry you have not been home from the hospital to know that we have had visitors. Rita, this is Dr. Kruger, he is here with the German army, but his purpose is to help expand the amount of services that are available at the hospital. Your Uncle Beppe invited him for dinner this evening, so we can get to know each other better. I have been having some pain in my leg lately, and he was kind enough to take a look at it for me."

"I am honored to meet you, Miss Rita Marron. I have been told that you are taking the nursing courses offered by the hospital, and that you are excelling at your studies." Dr. Kruger reached out and gallantly kissed Rita's hand, and bowed in respect, just as he had for Lucia and Anna. Rita smiled at both his polite attention and his kind words about her nursing. She was interested to hear he was a doctor, and wanted to hear all about how he came to be in Lake Braies.

Donna Lucia inclined her head and announced "Dinner is ready to be served. Conversation is always more pleasant over a good meal. If you will step this way, Doctor, we can be seated."

The meal was wonderful, and there were a great many things on the table that they had not enjoyed for quite some time. Beppe was curious, so he asked, "How is it that your Italian is so perfect, Doctor? I have seldom heard a German with such perfect pronunciation as yours."

"That is a good question, and I will be happy to share my story with you. I have always wanted to be a doctor, and I worked very hard, even as a child to make my dreams come true. My family supported my aspirations, even though no one in our family had more than a basic elementary education. I was fortunate to earn top marks in school, and through my family's sacrifice, and a partial grant, I was able to attend the University in Bologna. I graduated with a degree in Orthopedic Medicine, and I was at the top of my class. During my years at the University I fell in love with and married a wonderful young Italian woman. We returned to Germany after my graduation, and I set up my practice there. My wife and my two daughters live in Munich at this time, and I miss them very much. It was important to both my wife and I that our daughters retain their entire heritage, so we have insured that they speak Italian as well as German at home. That is why my Italian is so good; I still use it frequently with my family." Dr Kruger smiled at their surprised expressions, hearing about his Italian connection.

"Well, that explains it," laughed Guido, "You are half Italian!"

Everyone laughed, clearly enjoying Guido's joke. "It is good to be with you, and hear the pleasant Italian conversation around the dinner table; it feels like I am home again. There is another reason I am here, beyond my extreme fondness for the good wine of this country. No one can say how long this terrible war will drag on. I am here to add another wing onto the hospital in Lake Braies, and establish an Orthopedic Unit there. You yourself know the kinds of horrendous wounds that can result from combat, and I want to have the equipment and trained personnel here in Lake Braies in place to help with the casualties that we know will be coming. I have already sent dispatches to the German Government, outlining my plans and requests for equipment and supplies. I myself will spearhead the teaching of your local doctors in the latest techniques in Orthopedic Surgery, so they will be able to assist me when the casualties begin arriving. I am afraid that ours will be a very popular unit, and I am trying to get all the assistance that I can. The faster we can treat a traumatic injury, the better the outcome for the patient. The people of Lake Braies and the surrounding region will also benefit from this new wing. Count Donat, as the titled ruler of this region, I would like to ask your permission to proceed with my plans for the hospital." The doctor paused, clearly waiting for Beppe's permission, even though he had the might of the German Army at his back.

"You honor us with this ambitious plan, Dr. Kruger. We do indeed understand what can happen in war, and how important it is to treat the wounded quickly. Perhaps Guido would still have two legs if such a facility were closer when he was hit by shell fragments. Thank you for the courtesy of asking, and I am happy to grant you permission to add a wing onto the hospital to accommodate an Orthopedic Unit." Beppe was clearly pleased that the doctor had followed Italian protocol, instead of just forging ahead with his project like a German battleship.

"Thank you, Count Donat," I will inform my superiors that we have the clearances necessary to start building. I was wondering if I could secure some space in the hospital to begin training doctors, while the building is underway. I hate to lose any time in training, waiting on the building to be finished."

"I have no objections, but it would be best to take it up with the administration at the hospital, and get their full cooperation with your most worthy endeavor." Beppe replied, knowing the proper chain of command should be followed to make sure everyone was informed and in agreement.

Dr. Kruger turned his attention to Rita at that point, who had been sitting, absorbing all of the news about the changes that would be coming to the hospital. "Miss Marron, you are close to finishing your nurse's training, are you not?"

"That is right, Dr. Kruger, I am almost ready to graduate with my nursing degree. Why do you ask?" Rita was interested in the doctor's question.

"I would like to have some help to examine your father's leg more closely, and a trained nurse would be a big help to me," was his easy answer.

"Of course, I would be glad to assist you so you can give aid to my father." Rita rose, and followed the doctor into the study, with Guido trailing along behind with them on his crutches.

After carefully examining the stump of Guido's leg, from every angle, the doctor sat back and thought for a minute. "Who ever took care of you initially did a very good job; I don't believe I could have done any better myself."

"He was an American doctor working at the hospital in Trento, when I was brought in from the front lines. I was unconscious, so I don't remember too much about my operation, I just woke up with a shorter leg." Guido laughed, trying to lighten the mood.

"Well Alpino, I have some good news for you and some bad news as well. Which would you like to hear first?" Anna, who had been sitting close to Guido during the examination was alarmed by the doctor's words, and reached over to hold Guido's hand.

"Good news always makes bad new easier to bear, so I think I would like to hear the good news first. " Guido said, looking back at the doctor.

"The good news is that your leg will be all right, and the pain should go away pretty soon," Kruger said, with confidence in his voice.

"And the bad news, Doctor?" asked Anna, nervous about what he would say next.

"The bad news you will only live another sixty years or so. I wish I had gotten here sooner!" With that, everyone breathed a sigh of relief, and had another good laugh.

"Here I thought it was impossible for a German to have a good sense of humor," chuckled Guido. "You must be an exception, Doctor, because you are married to a nice Italian girl, so now you are half Italian!"

Rita was impressed with the doctor's abilities and his easy manner with Guido. She decided he would be a good person to stay close to, as he had a lot he could teach her. The soldier that the doctor had given the note to before dinner was back, and knocked at the front door. He handed the doctor a small package, and his medical bag, before turning and going back out the door. The doctor checked the contents of the package, and retrieved a syringe from his bag, preparing to give Guido an injection for his infection. Kruger noticed Rita's interest in what he was doing and asked, "Would you like to give your father his injection?"

Rita nodded immediately, grateful for a chance to learn a new skill, and to be able to help her father at the same time. "You will need to show me where you would like me to inject it, Doctor." Rita replied, concentrating on drawing the amount of antibiotic into the syringe that the doctor had directed.

"Probably the best site would be on his tongue," laughed the doctor, "But for now, right here above his knee." The doctor observed the professional manner in which Rita was able to inject the medication into her father's inflamed leg, without undue discomfort to him.

"That was very well done, Miss Marron," complimented Kruger. "Would you be interested in a position on my staff? I could use a person of your caliber who also speaks Italian."

Rita accepted promptly, glad for the opportunity to earn a salary, but more interested in the valuable experience she would be gaining under such a prominent doctor. They moved Guido to the sofa, so he would be more comfortable, and the effects of the injection finally set in, allowing him to drift off to sleep.

Everyone who attended that first dinner together learned a lot of valuable lessons. It isn't wise to judge a book by its cover, and patience and respect and sincerity can bridge some very wide gaps that people can build between each other. Perhaps if natural enemies could work together for common goals, there was hope for the world yet. It was too bad that the silver tongued orators, like the maniac in Berlin, were blinding a lot of good German's eyes. They couldn't see that he was sending them down a slippery slope to certain destruction. Before it was all over, a lot of good people would pay the price for their lack of vision.

Beppe and Donna Lucia extended another invitation to the doctor to come to dinner again, in the near future. The doctor checked on the peacefully sleeping Guido, as he got up to leave. He thanked them for their hospitality, and was grateful to have spent such a pleasant evening, far from the concerns of the war.

"This was the most pleasant evening I can remember since leaving my wife and daughters in Munich. Please let me know when you would like to do this again, and I will make sure that I hold a place open in my schedule for it. This reminds me of when I was young, and I was courting my wife. With so much misery crashing around us, it is nice to have something pleasant to think about for a while. I would like to take some measurements of Sergeant Marron's leg. We have made some great strides in the field of prosthetics in Germany in the last few years. I believe we can fit him with one that will be much more comfortable, and reduce the risk of infections in the future." Dr Kruger nodded his thanks, and headed out the door.

Chapter Fourteen

At this point I would like to interrupt my grandfather's tale, and relate something my father told me about that he witnessed when he was about eight years old. He was living on the Adriatic coast for a time, because of the war. The Germans were looking for young Italian men to help in the munitions factories, assembling bombs and rockets, destined for the aerial war over England. They even had plans to eventually cross the Atlantic and take the war to the American Continent. Anyone who refused to work in the factories would be sent to the concentration camps. My father's two older brothers, along with many other young men, didn't want anything to do with the Germans, and hid out in the surrounding farms and estates. My grandfather, a decorated soldier from the First World War, was home with my grandmother and my father. The German soldiers were mad because they were unable to find the young men. My grandfather wasn't able to walk very well because of his injuries in the war. The soldiers viciously hit his wounded leg with a rifle butt, before leaving the house empty-handed. My father never got over that sight, and he made sure I was told about it, many times over the years. It was hard for Italians to respect or trust Germans, so I found my grandfather's tale about cooperation with the German Army quite out of character, considering his own history with them.

The war was very hard on my father's family, and many times they didn't have enough to eat, and were weak from hunger. My father saw things that a small boy should never have to see. Children should see butterflies and kites, play ball, and read good books. Perhaps that is why it is so important to me to share my grandfather's story. It gives a human face to war, and the toll it can take on people. I am sure it is why he was always telling his tales of the war, while he and my father worked. If we can learn from our history, perhaps we won't have to live through it all over again.

Chapter Fifteen

As the war raged on, Rita became a trusted member of Dr. Kruger's staff. She worked very long hours to attend to all of the soldiers that had been injured in combat. The Orthopedic Wing was indeed as busy as the good doctor had predicted. The wards were overflowing with soldiers from both the Italian and the German Armies.

Rita was becoming a beautiful young woman, and she attracted the appreciative glances of many in the hospital, both staff and patients. When Rita wasn't on duty, she was at home with her family at the Castle. It was her private refuge from all of the ugly realities that surrounded her on a daily basis. She avoided the temptations of the handsome young men by staying busy in the gardens and riding her trusted horse Bianca. It was a great loss to her when her faithful companion died, leaving her without a good way to release the stress of her job.

Rita frequently spent time at her father's old apartment in town, instead of going all the way out to the Castle. It was closer to the hospital, and she could duck in there for a quick bite to eat, or a nap, easier than making the long trip to the other side of the lake on her bicycle. The apartment was a special place to her, and she found peace in the times she was there. She liked to sit in the old rocking chair by the fireplace, and try to imagine her birth mother, Maria, sitting there beside her. Rita was sad that she had never had the opportunity to meet her mother, and even though she had been surrounded by many wonderful women in her life. There was still an empty hole that would never be completely filled.

A few steps across the alleyway, Rita could visit her grandmother, Anna's mother. Rita had always had a special place in her heart for Grandma Delia, and visited her as often as she could manage. The dear woman doted on Rita, and she was a real comfort to her as she entered the autumn of her life. Grandma Delia would tell her about Maria, and how she used to come and visit her and Anna regularly.

"That was your mother's favorite place, when we would have a cold day," remarked Grandma Delia. "She would sit in that rocking chair, just like you are now, and gaze into the fireplace as the flames danced in the logs." The older woman coughed, with a sound that worried Rita.

"You should go to see the doctor with that cough; it doesn't sound very good to me." Rita looked at her adopted grandmother with real concern. "I will come and pick you up tomorrow. I will get you right in, you won't have to wait in line to see a doctor. I am friendly with all of the hospital staff, and they would be glad to have the opportunity to do me a favor."

"Thank you, my dear, you are such a comfort to me. Why don't we have a nice cup of tea? It is getting colder out, and I think a cup of tea would do me as much good as any of those fancy doctors!" The old woman laughed at her own joke, but it started her coughing again.

"Grandma Delia, I imagine you knew my mother as well as anyone in Lake Braies." ventured Rita, waiting for her to tell her more things about her mother.

"Yes, she was a lovely girl. She was a frequent customer at your father's and your grandfather's flower shop. She worked for Dr. Marron's family, and they were quite fond of having a great many fresh flowers in their home. We used to sit here in this room and do our embroidery together. That reminds me. I wonder if I still have that. Pardon me, while I take a look." Delia rose to her feet and walked over to an old trunk in the corner. She opened the lid and peered inside for a moment, moving a few things around. "Here it is," she called out with satisfaction, taking something out of the depths of the old trunk where it had sat for many years. She handed Rita a large fine square of white cloth that might have been a handkerchief at one time.

Rita unfolded the material carefully, not wanting to damage it because it appeared old. When it was open all of the way she could see that it had been lovingly embroidered, and there was a great deal of work on the square of cloth. It had the traditional hat of the Alpini soldier, with a long feather attached to it. The feather was very colorful, and was striking in its artistry. There was also a rifle, done in very fine detail, and it was being held by the arm of an angel. Rita just sat there, staring at the treasure in her hands.

"Your mother made that, after your father had left for the war. She spent hours and hours on it, as if somehow it might keep him safe. I suppose it was fate that it was meant to find its way back into your hands. I am sure that Maria would be happy knowing that you have it now."

Rita nodded gratefully for one of the few things that her mother had touched. She ran her hand over the needlework, marveling at its beauty. The feather seemed unusually long, and in Rita's imagination she could see her mother adding the extra stitching, as if somehow insuring a long life for the man she loved. She imagined the rifle in the angel's arms meant a quick and final end to the war.

"Thank you, Grandma Delia, I can't tell you what this means to me. Obviously my father never saw this; it will make him very happy when he sees it too." Rita had tears of gratitude running down her face, spilling onto the lovely legacy that her mother had left behind with an old friend. She wondered if Maria thought about that small piece of herself, when she left Lake Braies behind for the convent, without a word to anyone? Rita liked to think that she somehow knew that those she loved would find it one day, as her parting gift.

"What do you hear from Paul in Switzerland?" asked Grandma Delia, taking a sip from her teacup.

Chapter Sixteen

In Switzerland Paul Donat and his cousin Philip Von Strass continued their studies. They worked very hard, and studied together every spare minute of the day. The work didn't seem like work, they were so absorbed in the wonder of the things they were learning. It was not uncommon for one to break into the room on a dead run, with some amazing fact or other that they had just learned. They were highly regarded by all of their professors, and were not at all like some of the other privileged nobility that were attending the University. These young men really cared about what they were doing, not just taking a long expensive vacation, like some of the spoiled aristocrats they had encountered in their classes.

Sometimes it was hard to concentrate on their school work, as there was little news available from Italy. What small bits they could glean came from the British, the B.B.C. shortwave broadcasts. It was a puzzle to try and figure out what was true, and what was rumor or speculation. It was very frustrating for Paul, and he was worried about his family back in Lake Braies. He felt completely helpless sitting in Geneva, a world away from the fighting back home, but there was nothing he could do. He couldn't even go home for a short visit over the summers; it was far too dangerous to try and travel to Italy. All he could do was take extra classes with Philip, and try not to think about what might be happening back home. He would just have to call on the faith that had been a part of him, since his earliest memories in the beautiful little chapel near the Castle. God would have to take care of his family now. He would concentrate on becoming a doctor, and going home to help when this terrible war was over.

Philip was concerned for his cousin. With all of the work they had, Paul would still get up sometimes in the middle of the night and pace restlessly in their dorm room. Christmas vacation was approaching, and Philip decided a break would do them both good. His family had a chalet at a ski resort not too far from Geneva. Some skiing and the tranquility of the mountains would do them both a world of good. Paul was reluctant to go, feeling guilty about having fun, when he had no idea what was going on at home. Philip was a good friend, and convinced Paul that they would study much better if they took a break, and cleared their minds.

The mountains were breathtaking, in their pristine glory after another coating of snow from the last storm. The mountain almost sparkled in the first rays of the sun, inviting Paul and Philip to come and challenge her slopes. She could be soft, like the gentle touch of a mother's hand, with the snow flying up in their faces as they made their way down the mountain. Or, the mountain could turn into a demon, in a heartbeat. The deep mantel of a fresh snow could suddenly break free of the mountain and chase them down the slopes like all of the hounds of Hades itself.

Paul and Philip were both expert skiers, and knew the moods of the mountain, and were careful not to provoke her to anger. They skied, and took the tram back up to the top. Jumping off, they raced back down the mountain again, eager to reach the bottom, and begin the cycle all over again. The snow in their faces and the cold wind in their lungs helped them forget everything for a while. It was good just to react to the terrain, without thinking. Good to feel the freedom of the controlled drop down the steep slopes, barely in control, as the trees raced by.

After a long exhausting day on the mountain, Paul and Philip were sitting outside at a small café near the slopes, drinking mugs of hot tea, with a little brandy in it for extra warmth. The beauty of the panorama that spread out before them was something that you would never be able to forget. They could see a cloud of ice fog slowly creeping over the summit of the mountain. It wouldn't be very long before its icy fingers would reach out and halt all of the skiing for the day. Cold was one thing, and you could always put on extra clothes to keep warm, but fog was a different matter all together.

The skiers on the slopes were starting to make their way down, rapidly, knowing full well they didn't want to be stuck on the mountain side without being able to see their way down. Philip, the more experienced skier, was watching two skiers that had jumped off of the tram at the last minute, instead of riding it back down safely. The two skiers were racing ahead of the bank of fog that was pursuing them, and they were slowly losing the battle.

"Look at those two idiots," called Philip in alarm. "What do they think they are doing? They must be crazy trying to beat that fog to the bottom of the mountain. They might not be able to see the pine trees soon, but the pine trees will always know where they are, fog or not!"

Paul and Philip rose to their feet, trying to keep the two skiers in sight as long as they possibly could. The two were nearing their destination, when the fog finally overtook them, and they were lost from sight. The cousins strained their ears, trying to hear if they had made it safely down. They didn't have to wait very long before they heard frantic screaming somewhere off to the right, where they had last seen the two desperate forms.

"I knew it, I knew it!' Shouted Philip to Paul, as they rushed to see if there was something they could do to help. They joined other expert skiers in that terrible fog, unable to see more than a few feet in front of them. Somewhere they heard the voice of a female, clearly on the verge of panic.

"Help, please, won't someone help us? My sister is hurt!" Philip and Paul stayed close together, so they wouldn't get lost in the fog, too. It was difficult to tell where the cries for help were coming from, the fog made it seem like the sound was coming from everywhere, and all at the same time. They held on to each other, and concentrated on shuffling their feet, so they would be able to find their way back again. The screams were getting closer, and more urgent. It was clear that the woman was almost hysterical, calling out for someone to help her sister.

By some miracle, Philip and Paul stumbled upon the fallen sisters, almost literally. The two medical students immediately bent over the fallen sister, laying ominously still next to a large pine tree. It was clear that this was serious, and from the blood it appeared that the young woman had hit the tree head first. Philip knelt down and took his wool scarf off, and packed it with snow, wrapping it tightly around the woman's head, in an attempt to keep the swelling down. Paul was helping him straighten her body out, so they could prepare to lift her up off of the snow, when help arrived.

"What is your name?" Philip asked the sobbing sister, trying to distract her and help her focus on something else.

"My name is Lena, and that is my sister Janet. Our father is Professor Muller, and he teaches at the University. We are from Geneva," Lena added in a distracted voice. Her full attention was on her sister, or she wouldn't have had to add that they were from

Geneva, since there was only one university for miles around.

Paul caught the name, with a start, and asked "Would that be Professor Max Mueller?"

"Yes, he's our father, do you know him?" asked Lena looking up at Paul. Paul and Philip looked at each other, with awe clearly written on their faces. The fog was starting to lift a little, and the Ski Patrol spotted them, moving quickly in their direction to bring over a small snow sled used for moving injured skiers.

"Please be very careful with her head and neck, I think she may had hit the tree head first. Take her immediately to the hospital; she is going to need medical attention without delay!" Paul was shouting out the orders, allowing his training in emergency situations to take over, when his nerves were threatening to over whelm him.

The head of the Ski Patrol looked at Paul, and just shook his head. "We don't have a hospital here, just a clinic farther down in the valley."

"Well, the clinic is better than nothing, take her there immediately; every minute we lose getting her some help lessens her chance of survival." Paul spoke with such authority, that the Ski Patrol headed off for the clinic, as fast as they could safely go, pulling the sled with the inert woman behind them.

When they arrived at the clinic, there was no one there really qualified to handle an injury of this severity. The paramedics were there mostly to take care of cuts and bruises, and to help stabilize broken bones, until an accident victim could be transported to the hospital in Geneva.

"We are medical students from the University. I am Dr. Paul Donat, and this is my cousin Dr. Philip Von Strass. It is imperative that we speak to this young woman's father, Dr. Max Muller at the University. Please help us find the number, this is an emergency!"

The Paramedic on duty immediately looked through his emergency numbers, and dialed the University without delay. As the phone was ringing, he handed the phone over to Paul.

"Is this Dr. Muller?" asked Paul, nodding to Philip that he had reached the women's father. "This is Dr. Paul Donat; I am here at the resort clinic at Mt. Saleve. I am with my cousin Dr. Philip Von Strass; we are both students in your neurology class. There has been an accident and your daughter, Janet, has been injured. I believe she has sustained a serious head injury, when she hit a tree in the fog. She has considerable swelling on the right side of her head, and we packed her head in snow at the scene, in an attempt to reduce the edema. She has not regained consciousness, and there is no one here trained to handle this type of injury."

"Dr. Donat is there someone there who can assist you?" asked Dr. Mueller.

"Dr. Von Strass, can assist me, there are no nurses here. What did you have in mind?" There was growing unease in Paul's mind, as he thought about where Dr. Mueller was headed with this line of questions.

"I remember you Dr. Donat; you are one of the Neurology Interns enrolled in my program at the University. I am going to need you to draw on all of the information you have learned from me over the last three years, and drill a small hole in her skull to relieve the pressure that is building up. I am counting on you, because you are the only chance she has. I am leaving immediately, but if the injury is as bad as you think, the pressure will kill her long before I can reach her. Remain calm, son, and let your training take over. I will be there as soon as I can!" With that the doctor hung up and grabbed up his medical bag along with a special surgical bag, and headed for the door of his office. He had helped so many other injured people over the years; it was ironic that when a member of his own family was in dire need, he had to rely on a green intern from his own class to save her life. He prayed that God was awake and watching over these two young men, and Janet.

Paul hung up the phone, and stared at Philip, momentarily paralyzed with fear for what he had been ordered to do. "Well, Paul, what did Dr. Muller say?" Philip said uneasily, trying to read his cousin's expression.

"He said that we need to relieve the pressure that is building up inside Janet's skull as soon as possible. He is on his way, but he said this can't wait. She will be dead before he can get here, so it is up to us to do what is necessary to keep her alive. He said to focus on what he has taught us over the last three years, and our training would take over." Paul looked back at his cousin, marshalling his courage for what he must do.

"All right," nodded Philip, taking in the full scope of what they were about to do. "Let's get scrubbed and get set up. You are stronger in this area than I am, so I will back you up and assist. We should tell her sister that we have spoken to her father, and what needs to be done."

"I will see to getting things set up in the clinic, and you go talk to Lena, and fill her in on how her sister is doing." added Paul, already heading back to talk to the paramedic, and getting an area ready for the emergency surgery.

Philip found Lena, pacing back and forth in the room at the end of the hall. She rushed to him when she saw him coming, eager for word on Janet.

"How is my sister?" asked Lena, with a trembling voice.

"She has sustained a serious head injury from her impact with the tree. She is unconscious, and there is a great deal of edema—swelling—occurring. We are most concerned about the pressure that is building inside of her skull. If the pressure continues to build, it can do permanent brain damage, or kill her. We have talked with your father at the university, and he is aware of her condition. He can't make it here in time to take care of Janet; he feels she will be dead before he can arrive. My cousin, Paul, and I are your father's students. We have been in the neurology program for three years now, and your father has asked us to do the preliminary surgery necessary to reduce the immediate pressure, and stabilize Janet until he can get here to take over. With the bad weather he doesn't expect to arrive before morning. Paul will be performing the surgery, and I will assist him. We will let you know as soon as we are done, then it will be a matter of waiting to see if Janet will improve. After all we can do, everything is really in God's hands." Philip smiled at Lena, who was reluctant to let him go. He gave her a reassuring pat on her shoulder, and then headed off down the hallway after Paul, to get ready himself.

They had the small emergency area of the clinic as ready as they could make it. It was clean and well lit. They had the basics necessary to perform the surgery. Janet was on the examination table, draped with clean linen, and Philip was administering the anesthetic and monitoring Janet's vitals. He gave Paul the nod that he was ready for him, so Paul said a prayer for them all and reached for the scalpel.

The two cousins worked together, focusing on what they had been taught. Dr. Muller was correct; after the first few minutes of jitters from the realization of what they were doing, their training took over and they were able to do what was required of them. When Paul breached Janet's skull, the pressure released blood and fluid momentarily alarming both of them. It took several hours to complete their task, but they finished, and carefully wrapped Janet's head in gauze, and stepped back. They both removed their masks at the same time, exchanging a look that spoke of extreme fatigue and satisfaction. Now it was in God's hands. They had done all they could do for Dr. Muller's daughter.

"You go talk to her sister," said Paul, rubbing his tired eyes. "She will be worried, that it took longer than I expected. I will take the first watch and stay with her, while you try to get a little sleep. You can relieve me in two hours, and take over while I get some sleep. It won't do her any good if both of her doctors are so tired that they miss something that could be serious and impede her recovery."

"You're right, cousin," answered Philip, massaging his tired shoulders with one hand, and then the other. "I'll go talk to Lena and bring her up-to-date on Janet's condition. This has probably been hardest on her, since all she could do is wait in the other room and wonder what is going on in here. I'll see you in two hours."

Lena brightened immediately when Philip showed up; the look on his face immediately assured her that her sister was still alive and fighting for her life. "The surgery went well, and we were able to relieve the pressure. We can't really tell how much trauma she incurred during the collision with the tree, we won't know for a couple of days how bad it was. She is still in a coma, but her vital signs are strong and stable. Paul is taking the first watch, to monitor her condition, and I will relieve him in two hours. We will rotate through the night, until your father can arrive, and then he will assume her care. I suggest that you try to get some sleep as well; there isn't anything that you can do for her now, except pray. That's the most that any of us can do right now, wait and pray.

"Thank you for what you have done for us, Philip, I have been so worried. It was crazy of us to try and race the fog bank to the bottom of the mountain. We could see it starting to crest the top of the mountain as we were arriving at the turnaround station for the gondola. Janet and I have skied since we could walk, and we probably take more chances than we should. We are always trying to see how far we can push our luck when we race down the slopes. Neither one of us even hesitated when we saw the fog; we just jumped out of the tram and headed for the slope that was the fastest way down. We have skied that slope a thousand times before, and thought we knew every tree on the mountain. When the fog caught up to us we became disoriented, and it was hard to know exactly where we were. We kept calling to each other, and instead of slowing down, we went even faster, knowing the bottom of the slope wasn't far off. I thought we were going to make it, when suddenly I heard a terrible thud, and Janet quit talking. I stopped immediately, and tried calling her name, but she didn't answer. It felt like it took me forever to locate her in the fog. I believe I understand what it must be like to be blind. My heart stopped when I found her crumpled up like a rag doll next to that tree, and I just starting screaming for help. I couldn't think of anything else to do." Lena finally seemed to run out of words at that point, and sagged back into a chair behind her.

"We have all taken chances when we ski," replied Philip, "We know what we are risking in exchange for the rush we experience as we speed down the slopes. You can't blame yourself for Janet's accident. Things can happen to us even when we do everything right. Try and get some rest;

 We will wake you if there is any change in her condition."

Philip walked back up to the office of the clinic, and called his parents to tell them what had happened. He let them know that he and Paul would be staying the night, to keep an eye on their patient until her father could arrive in the morning. With that, Philip went back to the waiting area, sat down in a chair near Lena's, stretched out his legs, and nodded off to sleep.

The morning dawned beautiful and clear. There was no hint of the fog that had crept down the slopes yesterday, like a hunting predator looking for the careless and the unwary. The mountain was as it had always been, serene and majestic, covered in a mantle of sparking snow that shimmered like a coating of crushed diamonds in the first rays of light. It was neither good nor evil, it just existed and endured. Those who answered the call of the mountain were the ones who would be accountable for how they attempted to become part of it.

Dr. Mueller arrived a few hours after dawn, driving through the night to reach his stricken children. One was hurt, but both were injured. His daughters had always loved the mountain, and they were avid skiers. He had never worried about them, they were experts, and could take care of themselves. It still didn't seem possible, and he replayed the phone call over and over again in his head on the endless trip. In good weather, the trip from Geneva wasn't that long, but when the storms of winter descended, the trip could stretch into days.

Philip had just been relieved by Paul when their professor arrived at the clinic. Lena had finally dropped off to sleep a few hours earlier, when exhaustion had overtaken her. Dr. Muller recognized Philip immediately, and let his daughter sleep, while he got an update on Janet's condition.

"Good morning Dr. Muller," said Philip, extending his hand to his Professor, who shook his hand firmly and waited for Philip to brief him on his daughter's condition. "I am glad you have arrived safely, we were concerned because the roads have been very treacherous. Your daughter's surgery was completed about three hours after we spoke yesterday, and we are confident that the pressure was relieved. She was unconscious when we found her, and she has not been responsive since. Dr. Donat and I have taken shifts around the clock since her surgery to monitor her condition. Her vital signs have remained strong and stable, and she is still in a coma. I just left her a few minutes ago, and her condition has remained unchanged. Dr. Donat is in with her now. I am sure you would like to examine her and review her charts."

"Thank you, Dr. Von Strass. It has been a great comfort to me knowing the two of you were here. I find it ironic that I have helped so many people in a similar crisis over the years, but when my own daughter needed me, I had to rely on others for her care. It makes me better understand what it is like to stand and wait for word; it was a very helpless feeling. I would like to examine Janet now. We will let Lena sleep; she looks exhausted." Dr. Muller gave his sleeping daughter a smile, and turned his attention to his other daughter whose needs were more immediate at the moment.

Paul looked up when Dr Mueller and Philip entered the room. He stood and extended his hand to the man who had been a central figure in his academic life for the last three years. "Good morning, sir," Paul spoke, with a voice that was still a little unsure from a string of naps through the night. "Your daughter is stable, and her vital signs have remained unchanged. She is in a coma, but with the trauma that she has received as a result of her injury, I think that you would agree that it should be expected." Paul handed the tablet of paper they had borrowed from the clinic office to record their findings.

Dr. Mueller took the case file without hesitation and started to read the notes from surgery, as well the records of their observations through the night. When he had finished reviewing it, he laid it on the small table next to the bed, and examined his daughter. Even though he had been a doctor for many years, it was still difficult to see her there, with her head swathed in gauze. He noted that she also had two black eyes, and she may have broken her nose. It was evident from the scratches and bruises on her face that she had indeed collided head on with a tree. Her head must have been down and she was leaning forward when she made contact with the tree, as the top right side of her skull had taken the brunt of the impact. If she had hit the tree full face on, he doubted that she would have survived the impact.

He noted that the swelling seemed to be contained to the right side of her skull, and after checking her eyes, it was clear that she was in a coma. There was nothing to do now but wait and watch.

"Thank you, Dr. Donat, you have done a good job and have followed my instructions faithfully. I am gratified that you immediately packed her head in snow, in an attempt to mitigate the onset of the swelling. It probably saved her life, by delaying the pressure build-up until you could open her skull. If the pressure had been allowed to build up unchecked, we probably wouldn't be having this discussion. In cases such as these, it is difficult to assess the amount of damage that has occurred. There most certainly has been bruising to the brain, as evidenced by the swelling and coma. We won't be able to assess her cognitive functions until she regains consciousness. You have both done a magnificent job, under very difficult conditions. That is what medicine is all about; doing the best you can with what you have to work with. The rest is our skill and experience, and the hand of God resting on our shoulder."

Dr. Muller, satisfied that his daughter was stable and well cared for, headed out the door, to go render aid to his other daughter. As he entered the little waiting room, Lena was just starting to stir. She saw her father and jumped up to meet him, hugging him like she were a small girl again. "Oh Papa, I am so glad you are here. I am so sorry, this was my fault entirely. We should never have taken such a foolish risk, just to race the fog down the mountain on the final run of the day! How is Janet? Is she going to be all right?" Seeing her father had brought the tears back that she had just managed to get under control a few hours ago. She felt better knowing he was here, he was such a good doctor she was positive that he wouldn't let anything happen to Janet.

"It wasn't your fault, my dear," smiled her father, knowing both of his daughters were never afraid to push the limits of whatever it was they were doing. They egged each other on, and it was only the luck of the draw that Janet found a tree in the fog instead of Lena. "The two of you have been fearless since you could walk. If there was something that was beyond your reach, you would figure out how to grab it. It is the beginning of wisdom when you consider what could have happened, and are more prudent in the future. Janet is in a coma, but she is stable and not in any danger for the moment. We won't know how extensive her injuries are until she opens her eyes, and can talk to us. I am going to stay here and monitor

Janet, I want you to go back to your apartment and get some rest. I will call you if there is any change. I'll get Dr. Von Strass to take you home, and Dr. Donat will stay here with me."

Philip drove Lena back to the apartment she and her sister used during the skiing season. He was keeping a close eye on her, knowing that when someone has suffered a severe shock, it can manifest itself many hours later.

"Thank you for all you have done to help us, Dr. Von Strass. I was crazy with fear when you and you cousin showed up. Yours was the first face I saw after I found Janet, and you just seemed to step in and take charge. I wasn't even thinking about what I should be doing for her, but you just took off your scarf and packed her head in snow. Being around my father all of these years, we have picked up what to do in an emergency, but my mind just went blank. Papa said you both did a good job helping her survive the initial injury. It is so hard waiting, not knowing how she is really doing. How could we have been so crazy?" Lena buried her head in her hands, as if trying to block out the consequences of their foolish impulse to race the fog.

"We got to her pretty fast, and the faster you can start treating a head injury, the better your chances of reducing any long-term damage. It wasn't your fault, so it is pointless to blame yourself. My cousin Paul and I are always trying to outdo each other on the slopes too. I think it is just human nature. I think that we have been through enough that it would be better if you called me Philip, Dr. Von Strass sounds like my father!" Philip smiled at her, hoping she could appreciate his joke. For her part, Lena laughed, and gave him a hug. It felt good to have someone to lean on, when the world seemed to tilt off of its axis at the moment. Lena released her hold on Philip, but continued to hold his hand until they reached her door. He had been there when she needed a friend, and she felt like she had known him forever.

Dr. Muller stayed to see that Janet was transported safely to the University Hospital in Geneva, while Paul and Philip headed back to the Palace. Philip's parents were waiting for them when they arrived, and were eager to hear all of the details of the accident. They were proud of both Paul and Philip for the way they were able to respond to the emergency. They were sure it was no accident that these two young doctors were there to render assistance in a difficult situation. How amazing that they were able to use what they had been taught to save a life, and they had not even finished their internship.

The two cousins ate a big meal, having had nothing to eat since some tea just before the accident occurred. Then they trudged up the big staircase and headed for a hot shower. They got a few hours of sleep, and then prepared to head back to the University.

Philip was already downstairs when Paul made his way down the stairs. Some times a little sleep was worse than no sleep at all. Paul's head felt like it was stuffed with soggy cotton, and it was hard to pull his thoughts together.

"It must have been terrible for the girl's sister," remarked Philip's mother, after hearing more about the Muller family. "I would have been out of my mind with worry, if something like that had happened to one of my sisters."

"Lena was pretty shaken up, but I did the best I could to reassure her it wasn't her fault. I'll probably look in on her again, to see how she is doing. After a shock like that it is good to have someone to talk to. Since Paul and I were there from the time it happened, it is easier to share your thoughts and fears with someone who knows what you went through." Philip confided to his parents.

"We are so grateful the two of you worked so well together, Paul." said his uncle, with pride shining in his eyes. 'It is not every day that you are able to take charge of an emergency, and use the skills and experience you have learned to change what surely would have resulted in that poor woman's death. I wish Beppe and Guido could be here right now, they would both be so proud of you. They know what it is like to have to depend on others to make the right decisions to save a life!"

"Thank you, Uncle," replied Paul, not really impressed with his own actions. "I just did what anyone else would have done, in our situation. Philip was the one who had the presence of mind to pack her head in snow to slow down the swelling, and keep it from being as bad as it could have been. I was very glad he was there; it really helped to keep me steady and focused on what Dr. Mueller had taught us."

"We are going to head back to the University. I don't know when Dr. Muller and his daughters will arrive, so our usual classes will probably be cancelled since Dr. Muller will be busy today. There are still a lot of things to do, and we can make rounds with one of the other residents. I hope Dr. Muller has called and left word on how Janet is progressing. It might be a good idea if we stop by the flower shop on the way, and pick up some flowers. Those rooms at the hospital can be a pretty gloomy place," finished Philip, thinking out loud. His Aunt gave Paul a knowing smile, since Philip's mind was a million miles away.

Paul and Philip were on hand when the ambulance carrying Dr. Muller and his daughters arrived later in the afternoon. The staff had been alerted, and a room was ready and waiting for Janet. The transfer went smoothly, and she was on a gurney as the nurses began taking her vital signs, and writing down Dr. Muller's instructions. Lena was standing over in the corner of the room, feeling a little out of place, wishing she had something to do, too.

Philip spotted her, and came over with the flowers they had picked up on the way to the hospital. "How are you feeling this afternoon, Lena," asked Philip, as he handed her the flowers. "We thought you might enjoy something pretty to lighten up this dull old room."

Lena was relieved to see Philip, and walked over to take the flowers. "I am well enough. There hasn't been any change in Janet's condition. It was hard to sit next to her all the way back to Geneva in the ambulance. She looks too beat up and pale, almost like a stranger instead of my sister. I kept watching her chest rise up and down, to assure myself she was still alive. I am not used to seeing her like this; she is always so active and full of fun." Lena found a forgotten vase to put the flowers in, and went over to the sink to fill it up with water. "Thank you for the flowers, it will be nice when Janet wakes up to have something pretty for her to look at."

Paul was standing behind Dr. Muller, observing as the doctor supervised the transfer of his daughter into her bed. He noticed that the gauze had been changed since the last time he saw her, but little else appeared to be different.

Dr. Muller came over to speak to Paul as soon as he was free. "She tolerated the ambulance ride back to Geneva well. Her vital signs haven't changed since you and Dr. Von Strass left her yesterday. I am glad to have her back at the University Hospital; in case anything should arise, we are much better equipped to deal with it here. You did a fine job on taking down her swelling and relieving the pressure. I had a better chance to examine your work when I changed her dressings this morning. There is some leakage from the incision, but that is to be expected. She may be in one of the top facilities in the world now, but there is still nothing more we can do for her than we could at that little clinic. It is all up to her and God now, so we will be patient and wait."

Chapter Seventeen

Two days later, Paul was checking on his patient again, when she started to stir. He had brought some fresh flowers to replace the ones that had been there when she arrived. She slowly opened her eyes, and tried to focus on her surroundings. She looked at the man standing next to her bed with some flowers in his hand and asked "Who are you? Where am I?" Janet looked confused, but not frightened.

"You are in the University Hospital in Geneva. You had a skiing accident three days ago. You got lost in the fog coming down the mountain, and crashed into a tree. I am Dr. Paul Donat. My cousin, Dr. Philip Von Strass, and I were also skiing at the resort when your accident occurred. It is good to see you awake and talking. I am going to call your father and your sister, they will be anxious to see that you are awake."

The nurse came into the room, and Paul left Janet in her care while he went to summon Dr. Muller. He found him in his office, buried behind an impressive amount of paperwork on his desk. The doctor looked up as Paul stuck his head in the door, with momentary alarm showing on his face. "It is all right, doctor" began Paul, in a reassuring tone. "I was just checking on Janet, when she started to stir. She is awake and asking for you. I left her with the duty nurse and came to find you immediately."

"Thank God!" exclaimed Dr. Muller, with a sigh of relief. "It has only been three days, and while that is not uncommon in such cases, for me it has seemed like a lifetime!" He rose to his feet and made haste for his daughter's room. "Dr. Von Strass took Lena down to the cafeteria to get some coffee. Would you be so kind as to go down there and let them know that Janet is awake? Lena has really been tormenting herself since the accident, and it will help her to see her sister's eyes open."

Paul found Philip and Lena sitting at a table in the hospital cafeteria, having a cup of coffee and talking to pass the time. Lena spotted Paul first, and was immediately on her feet, moving in his direction. Philip wasn't far behind, trying to read the expression on Paul's face.

Paul held his hand up, while they were still half way across the room, to signal that everything was okay. "Don't worry, everything is all right, I just wanted to let you know Janet is awake. Dr. Muller is with her now, and he asked me to come down and find you and let you know."

Lena gave a nod of relief, and turned to lean against Philip for a moment. "This has been the longest three days of my life. Is she able to talk? Does she know what happened?" Lena was looking at Paul, waiting for more information, so she could try and understand how her sister was doing. Philip just stood close by her, for moral support.

"She can see; she was looking around the room. She can speak; she wanted to know who I was, and where she was. I gave her the basics, and went to get Dr. Muller. She was talking to the duty nurse when I left. I am sure she would like to see you, Lena, you can answer a lot more questions for her than we can." Paul held the door open to the cafeteria, and the three of them headed upstairs to Janet's room.

When they walked into the room, Dr. Muller was sitting on the edge of her bed, hugging her. In spite of being one of the top doctors in the hospital, he was a father first and his daughter's state of mind was the most important thing to him at the moment. Janet caught sight of her sister as she came into the room, and immediately reached out a hand for her. Janet went around to the other side of the bed, and gently hugged her sister, afraid she might injure her further. Paul and Philip stood back and watched the family reunion with satisfaction and relief. It was a validation that they had chosen the right career. The long hours of study, and the nights they postponed sleeping and eating trying to cram everything into a day suddenly seemed a very small price to pay. To be sure they would have many similar experiences ahead of them, in the years to come, but this was special because it was the first time that theory had been translated into reality.

"Gentlemen, if you would care for a proper introduction," Dr. Muller was turned towards them, and motioned for them to come closer to the bed. "Janet, these are two of my best interns, Dr. Paul Donat, and Dr. Philip Von Strass. It was very fortunate for you that they enjoy skiing, too. If it had not been for their quick actions following your accident, we might very well have had an entirely different outcome."

"Thank you for what you did for me. I am afraid I don't remember any of you, but I was lucky that fortune favors the foolish. Thank you for looking after my sister for me. I can imagine how I would have felt if it had been her who hit the tree instead of me. I would also like to thank you for the flowers; it was very thoughtful of you to even think of it. I am sure my father must keep you pretty busy, he doesn't believe in working his Interns any less than he works himself." Janet attempted to smile, but it was clearly an effort for her.

"You look much better with your eyes open," said Paul with obvious relief that his efforts seemed to have made a difference. "Someone with such beautiful eyes should make it a point to try and keep them open as much as possible." Everyone laughed at his joke, feeling the relief that she seemed to be doing well in spite of all that she had gone through.

"I feel like I know you already," said Philip, and he gently took Janet's hand. "Lena has talked about nothing but you since I met her. If I have a test on your early childhood, I shall pass easily!" Janet gave Lena a glare, wondering what her sister had been telling compete strangers. She made a mental note to grill her on the subject later.

As Janet was sitting up in bed, she felt a little dizzy, and she had a terrible pounding headache. Paul was the first to notice the look of discomfort that passed on her face. "Are you in pain?" he asked stepping in to take a closer look. Her father was right at his side, looking into her eyes.

"I think you have had enough excitement for one day, young lady," said Dr. Muller as he examined her eyes more closely. "I am going to give you something for the pain; it will help you relax and get some rest. I will be here when you wake up." He filled a syringe with a clear liquid, and gently injected the contents into her arm. "Rest now, my dear, I will see to it that your Guardian Angels are around if you should need anything."

Janet smiled and slowly closed her eyes, listening to the voices around her as she drifted off to sleep. Everyone headed toward the door, to let her get the rest that was as important to her recovery. Lena leaned down and kissed Janet on the cheek, trying hard not to notice all of the discoloration on her skin from the accident.

"Gentlemen, if I might have a moment of your time?" Dr. Muller motioned for Paul and Philip to come over. "Dr. Donat, I know this is a particularly busy time for you, with final exams just around the corner. I would appreciate if you would include regular visits to check on Janet, since technically she is your patient. I will see to it that your other professors are informed of your extra duties, you won't be penalized for the additional time you spend here."

"Dr. Von Strass, it has meant a great deal to Lena that you have found the time to help her through these particularly trying few days. So much attention is focused on the patient that someone who has been part of a bad accident can be completely overlooked. Lena and her sister have been particularly close since their mother passed away. Lena has felt so lost and guilty, and I haven't had the time to spend with her as I would have liked. You have really filled in for me, and I want you to know that I appreciate it. If you can make yourself available from time to time, it is important for a person's mental health to be able to open up and talk about their feelings and fears. That is the best way to ensure such feelings don't build up and overwhelm you." With that Dr. Muller headed out the door, aware that there were a lot of other people who needed him too. He felt better knowing that these two young men would help him in the days ahead.

In the busy days that followed, Paul and Philip took to heart their Professor's request. Philip was a frequent visitor to Lena, and they soon learned each other's schedules. Lena felt so comfortable with Philip, and he helped her work out the doubts that still troubled her mind over Janet's accident. They would sit and talk in the cafeteria when they could find a few minutes in common. Each began to look forward to the few minutes they could carve out of their busy lives. Philip and Lena seemed to fit each other like a perfectly matched set of fine gloves. It was as if the mountain had watched the two of them ski, and decreed that they should be together.

Paul looked in on Janet several times a day, and was pleased on those occasions when she was awake. They talked about her injury, and how she was feeling. She still had no memory of the accident, but Paul assured her that her short term memory loss was normal. Janet looked at Paul with the special eyes of a person who had been privileged to actually meet their Guardian Angel. They built a real friendship as she slowly recovered. It was also not uncommon for a bond to form between a doctor and a patient. The bond between the broken and a healer can come fast, and appear without either of them noticing.

Paul was troubled by his emerging feelings for Janet Muller. He was still in love with Rita, but it had been so long since he had seen her, or even heard from her. He had no idea how Rita felt about him, and there was no question that Janet adored him. There was no word out of Italy, but the papers were filled with news as the war was intensifying, crashing over his country. Janet was here, and it was easy to forget when he was in her company that there was still another life back in Lake Braies. He felt confused, and disloyal, but it seemed it was possible for the human heart to love more than one person.

Chapter Eighteen

Back in Lake Braies, Rita was still working for Dr Kruger, and working every moment her eyes were open. Even with all of the women that were currently training at the Nurses Program at the hospital, they were still critically short handed. There were volunteers from the town, and nuns helped out from a Convent, but there were never enough hours in the day. Every day there were new casualties to take care of. The ones who were stable were moved to other facilities where they could convalesce. The Orthopedic Unit was always a hive of activity, treating the most critically wounded first.

There were some patients who were too far gone to be helped by the surgical staff. The nurses that were technically off duty would make it a point to sit with them, to make their last hours easier. They would read to them, or talk to them, or listen to them, or write last letters to loved ones from their hometowns. There was always one more patient to see to, one more bed to be changed, and one more bag of personal belongings to gather up. These were taken to the person who ensured that these precious last mementos of the fathers, husbands, brothers, uncles, or cousins reached the people who most needed them. It was mentally exhausting, and you could lose your faith in God if you weren't careful, and your soul would die.

Rita tried to stay busy mentally, not thinking about Paul so far away in Switzerland. She knew he was probably safe, because Switzerland was a neutral country. It was a place where people from all over the world could still sit down at the same table and talk, without the fear of someone shooting at them. She frequently stayed in town, because she didn't have the luxury of going home to the Castle every night. Once in a while she would see her father or her mother, or her Uncle or her Aunt when they happened to be in town. She spent as much time as she could with Grandma Delia, but there was still a terrible emptiness in her. She needed a friend, someone she could talk to and share her feelings with. That would have been Paul, when he was still at home, but it had been over three years since she had seen her best friend. That best friend had somehow become something more, right before he left for the university. It still confused her, and she didn't know how she felt. She knew it would be the happiest day in their lives for her family, if she and Paul were to marry. Her father and Anna seemed happy, but there was still sadness in her father's eyes that she caught every now and then. He had cried when she had shown him the embroidered cloth that Grandma Delia had given her. He loved Anna with all of his heart, but there was a greater happiness he might have had, if her mother had lived. She would very much like to have a love like that, but perhaps happy should be enough for her. God knows there was so little happiness in the world right now. She didn't have time to think about Paul, and where he was right now, and what he was doing. There would be time later, when this war was over, and he came home to Lake Braies.

The casualties were steadily increasing as the battles intensified. Rita didn't always get to work with Dr. Kruger, because there was so much to do. She was one of the best nurses on the staff, in spite of her age. She had the sad benefit of too much practical experience in too short of a time. The hospital regularly got new doctors assigned, as other hospitals farther away from the front could spare them. One of the new arrivals was a young surgeon who specialized in internal medicine. He had been sent from the hospital in Trento, where her father and her Uncle had received treatment. He was blond, and stood out among the darker haired doctors from the region. He had attended the University in Milan, and was familiar with the very latest surgical techniques. He was much in demand, and Rita had the opportunity to work with him on several occasions. His name was Dr. Renato Pini, and his reputation for excellent work while under pressure attracted the attention of Dr. Kruger.

Dr Kruger liked to post the best surgeons in the Orthopedic Unit, so Dr. Pini found himself working there with increasing frequency. When there were breaks, he and Rita would talk in the lounge, while they grabbed a bite to eat, or steeled themselves for the next onslaught with a strong cup of coffee or tea. It was normal that they would discuss patients, and how they were progressing. Dr. Pini would explain about a certain technique that Rita had observed, and answer her questions. He would laugh at her interest, as none of the other nurses seemed to bother. He said she was wasted in the Nurse's Pool, and she should seriously consider becoming a doctor.

It was nice having someone to talk to, someone who encouraged her and who was confident in her skills. He was easy to be with, and he always had something to say that could distract her from all of the pain and misery that surrounded her. The pressures of war and the emptiness in her soul was a dangerous combination. She was learning the same lessons that Paul was learning, miles away in Switzerland. The heart could not be denied for ever; when it was empty it found a way to satisfy its loneliness. And like Paul, Rita discovered for herself that the heart could indeed love more than one person.

Paul had the advantage that Geneva was a very large city, and the people who walked its busy streets hadn't known him as a little boy. Rita had to be very careful about spending time with Renato outside of the hospital. Everyone knew her, and there was nowhere she could go that someone wasn't watching her. She just wanted to spend some time with him, and forget for a little while what her life was really like. She tried not to think about the slippery slope she was heading down, but she was only human. Rita wouldn't be able to avoid what was staring back at her every day.

Dr. Kruger noticed the close bond that was developing between two of the best members of his surgical team. He had a different view of such things than most people might. As long as their friendship didn't interfere with their work, he didn't care. He understood the pressures his staff was under, and he couldn't begrudge them a little happiness in the middle of so much sorrow.

After one particularly brutal day, with so many casualties that the staff lost count, it finally came to a head. Rita and Renato went for a walk to try and clear their heads. It was a beautiful night, and they just walked without any destination on their minds. They talked about anything and everything, just to avoid thinking about what they had been through today. Tomorrow would probably be more of the same, and there was no end in sight.

They finally found themselves at the end of the narrow street where Rita's father had his small apartment. It had been a long day, and without really thinking about it Rita invited Renato in for a cup of tea. It was quiet and familiar, and the fire from the stove was reassuring. They drank several cups of tea before they ran out of things to say. It had been a long time since Rita spent that special night with Paul, and the barriers she had built up around her. Her empty heart finally came crashing down. She never meant to betray Paul, but her heart just swept her away. For the first time in her life, Rita experienced what it was like to be in love, really in love.

Rita was more confused now than ever. She was standing on a battle field of her own making, surrounded by two warring factions. One carried the banner of her lifetime of friendship and love and loyalty for Paul. He had always been there for her, and been her brother and her confidant. There was nothing she could tell him that would make him think any less of her. She was honored that he loved her, and she felt no shame in what they had shared together.

The other faction carried the banner of her new love, Renato. They had not known each other nearly so long, but time seemed unimportant to the intensity of their bond, as they fought a battle for men's lives on a daily basis. They worked shoulder to shoulder trying to stand in the path of the Angel of Death, as he stalked the corridors of the wards. Renato was new and exciting and he believed in her. They had not grown up together, so there was no mistaking her attraction for him, as that of a beloved brother. She felt battered and beaten by both sides, as she stood there on the battlefield in her mind, cheering for both banners, and unable to wish for a victor.

It had been easier for her mother, she had loved one man, and only one man with all of her heart. She went to her grave loving him, and had left behind all that she had to give him, in the form of her only child. Rita wished she could talk to her mother now, and listen to what advice she might offer her. She could talk to Anna, of course, or even her Aunt Lucia, or her Grandma Delia. All three women would listen, these women loved her without reservation, but somehow it wouldn't be the same. She could never discuss this with her father or Uncle Beppe. They would not love her any less, but she knew they each cherished the secret hope that she would marry Paul some day, and make the final link in their family complete.

She finally decided to take her confusion to the place where she might receive her answer and bring this battle to an end. She would appeal to God for His help, and hopefully hear His counsel in the form of the mother Superior. She had visited the mother over the years, and all of the nuns who had helped to raise her. Uncle Beppe and father had kept their promise to bring Rita for visits, so it remained a place of comfort and peace for her. With all of the trouble in the world, it had not been possible to go since the war started. She knew she was due some time off soon, so she decided to ask Dr. Kruger if she might have a day to visit the Convent.

Dr Kruger knew how hard she had been working, and he thought it was a good thing to visit the Convent, hopefully finding the peace that the whole staff was so desperately in need of. The doctor agreed to let her have the time off, and arranged for her to make the trip in his black Mercedes. She had thought about asking Renato to drive her up, but as she thought about it, this was probably better. It would do nothing to clear her mind and reflect on the course her life should take, with the handsome young doctor sitting next to her for the hours it would take to travel to the convent and back. This was probably a sign from God that if she needed to hear His will, it was best not to bring too much noise with her.

"I hope you have a good trip, my dear," said Dr. Kruger as he helped her into the back seat of the big Mercedes. "It is very dangerous these days; I hope you don't mind that I am sending along two of my most trusted guards. I would hate to lose such a valuable member of my surgical staff, when you are needed here so badly. I hope the day at the convent will do you some good I know you have been troubled lately, and it is a good place to find some inner peace for a time. I will see you when you get back." With that the doctor signaled to his driver, and they headed out of the parking lot of the hospital, and on to the main road.

It was quiet in the car as they drove, the glass that separated the front seat from the back seat being rolled up. Rita had time to think, and to remember, and to ponder. There was no clear road ahead for her, and she only seemed to be going in circles. She bounced back and forth between what she felt and what she knew. There had to be an answer to this problem, she just had to have the courage to wait for the answer to find her.

The Mercedes had made short work of the road to the convent, and Rita was standing on the steps in front of the familiar old door before she knew it. She reached out and pulled the cord for the bell. She had always loved the sound of this bell when she was a child. It didn't ring very often, but when it did it usually meant that they were going to have some interesting visitors. She still remembered the day that the bell had brought her a father and an uncle. She hoped that the sweet sound of the beautiful little bell would be as lucky for her today. The small window in the door finally opened, and she could see the form of a Sister from the darken interior. It took a moment for Rita to make out the face on the other side of the door, but she finally recognized Sister Chiara.

"Hello, Sister Chiara, do you remember me? It's Rita." Rita waited for the aging nun to get a good look at her.

"Of course, Rita, is it really you! You are the treasure of my heart. You have grown into a real beauty; you look so much like your dear mother. It has been quite a while since we have seen you—please come in." The old nun hugged her, like a long lost daughter, and perhaps she was. "All of the Sisters will be so excited that you are here. They are at their personal prayers just now, but I can't believe God would be angry with them, if they came out and received this special blessing he has sent them." With that the tiny nun produced a small silver bell from her pocket, and began to ring it vigorously as they walked down the arched corridor towards the garden. Answering the call of the bell, the doors along the hallway began to swing open, and their occupants emerged. It didn't take them very long to understand the reason for the unexpected summons, and they hurried in Rita's direction to greet her. In a short time Rita was surrounded by a familiar sea of black and white, all intent on giving her a kiss and a hug. It was like being wrapped in love and Rita's tears didn't need much encouragement to wash her cheeks. She felt the peace of this place surround her, and welcome her into its loving arms. She felt like a small child again, with an army of mothers that loved her. She had been right to come here, and she felt certain that the answer that had eluded her in Lake Braies would find her here.

When the hugs and greetings finally slowed down, Rita began looking around for the mother Superior. Surely she had heard the bell announcing guests; perhaps she was delayed in her office. "I was hoping to talk to mother Superior," Rita started to say, and was shocked into silence when the Nuns suddenly all bowed their heads and made the sign of the Cross.

"My dear," spoke Sister Teresa gently, "Mother Superior, Sister Benedettina, is now with the angels in heaven. I have assumed her calling and mantle, but I will never be able to fill her shoes. She loved you as much as any Sister here, perhaps more. You were always in her heart and in her prayers. She rejoiced in your happiness, and in your life. She had hoped to see you one final time before she answered our Lord's call to return home. She was sure you would return here, looking for her, so she left you this final letter. I have kept it, since her passing, knowing she would be right." The woman who was now the new Mother Superior carefully drew the final commission from that dear friend and placed it into Rita's trembling hands. The rest of the Sisters tenderly touched her on the shoulder, as they went back to their rooms to pray for their departed Sister.

Rita walked slowly to her favorite bench, under a wooden arch, and considered the plain white envelope in her hands. She remembered her father telling her about a similar letter he had received from her mother. Her mother had written to him, not even knowing if he were still alive. Mother Superior had left her a letter, secure in the knowledge that Rita, too, would be able to read her final words. The symmetry was perfect, and this must be why she had been inspired to come here. She finally opened the letter, and began to read the words out loud to herself, as if the mother Superior was here in the garden with her.

My Dear Rita,

If you are reading these words, then the dearest desire of my heart has been answered. I had hoped that I might see you one final time, but I don't think that will be a blessing that I can count as mine. Your mother, Maria, wrote to your father, when she knew she was dying, and I have to believe it gave her a great deal of peace. I hope you are happy, my heart, and have found fulfillment in your life. If you have not, I would like to hold you in my arms one last time, and kiss all of your hurts away, like I did when you were young. The road to God can take us on many paths, as we stumble in the darkness to find Him. I hope it will comfort you to know that He is aware of you, and always knows where you are, even if you don't. Keep looking for Him, and you will find Him in the place you least expect. Pray always to stay close to Him, and follow the Ten Commandments. Be honest with yourself, and with those who love you. Allow God to speak to your heart, in the quiet moments, and listen to what it tells you. Confide the desires of your *heart to God, and believe that He loves you, and knows what is best for you. He will lead you on the road that will bring you back to His loving arms.*

I will always be there watching over you, as will your dear mother. We will rejoice in your victories, and pray for you in your trials.

I remain as I have always been,

Your Loving Mother Superior,

Sister Benedettina. "

Sister Teresa was watching Rita's expression, as she read the letter. To be sure there were tears; the final words of someone she loved deeply had touched her heart. But when she had finished, and had laid the letter in her lap, her face was blank and troubled.

"My Dear, clearly there was something important that you needed to discuss with the mother Superior, since you made such a long trip in these dangerous times. It does not seem to me that those last thoughts that she shared with you were the answers and the comfort you were hoping for. You are the daughter of every Sister here, and we thank God every day for the blessing He granted us in allowing us to raise you. You will always be our child; won't you allow us to share your burden with you, and tell us what is troubling you?" Sister Teresa looked at Rita with the eyes of a parent aching to give love and support to a child in pain.

"You are right, mother. I have reached a time in my life where I don't know what to believe any more. Everything was always so clear and simple, and I didn't have to give any thought to what was right and what was wrong. Now I don't know, and the road before me is dark and full of unexpected twists and turns. I need the counsel of the Sisters, and the benefit of their combined wisdom." Rita looked at the new mother Superior with the eyes of a drowning person, seeking something substantial to grab on to.

"We shall all assemble in the Chapel, and hear your words there. We will listen, with God, and pray to hear His wisdom."

The bell was sounded again, and the Sisters appeared from their cells, and began moving along the corridors in the direction of the Chapel. The room was a simple one with plain white walls and statues dotting the interior. The benches were plain wooden pews, and they had been worn smooth over the years, as countless bodies had occupied them to pray and to meditate. The Sisters assembled in the Chapel, and filled the benches to capacity. They sat quietly, with expectant faces looking at the mother Superior, ready to hear the reason for this gathering.

Rita was sitting at the front of the group, trying to organize the chaos in her mind. She loved and trusted everyone in this room, but she still found it difficult to assign words that would be able to share the ache in her heart.

"Sisters," began mother Superior, "we have come together to pray and to listen this morning. Our treasured jewel has come home to seek comfort and answers to the things of the world that threaten to overwhelm her. Let us pray, and ask the father of us all to open our minds and our hearts to allow us to listen and consider."

The nuns each bowed her head, and picked up the prayer beads hanging at their sides. There was no amount of time given for them to complete their preparations, it was just silent as each woman presented her petition to God. After a long pause, Rita finally felt ready to stand and unburden her soul in front of those who had loved her from the day she was born. She felt no shame, and her words were plain, and direct. She spared no details in describing the war she was experiencing in her soul. She talked of the two combatants, one a brother, and one a lover. She described the forces of duty and loyalty and obligation that pulled her in one direction, and the equally strong forces of love and attraction and fulfillment that pulled her in the other direction. She could make no headway in deciding which tether to cut, but if she didn't make a decision, the forces would rend her in two and destroy her completely. Spent and exhausted from the effort to reach out for help and council, Rita walked out of the Chapel and went to sit in the garden.

The Sisters looked at each other; this was a very difficult problem indeed. Each of them long ago had decided to forgo the option of a husband and a family in order to serve the Lord in this quiet sanctuary. Now someone they all loved desperately needed their wisdom on a subject they had no knowledge of, or experience with. They spoke quietly among themselves, in small groups, talking and listening in turn. They tried to match the question against the standard of their faith, and look to God for the conformation that they had applied it correctly. It was not easy, and they carefully considered every point that Rita had made in outlining her dilemma, but at last they were satisfied with their answer for her. One of the Sisters rose and left the chapel, going to find Rita. Rita looked up as the Nun approached; relieved that at last she might put an end to this struggle that had brought her to the brink of her sanity. Rita stood without a word and accompanied the Sister back into the chapel. The Sisters were all standing in a loose circle, and Rita took up her post in the middle of them as if she were protected on all sides.

"My dear," intoned mother Superior with a gentle smile on her face, "as you know we in this Order made a decision long ago to leave the secular world behind, and devote our lives to prayer and the service of God. We are protected in this small paradise of peace and contemplation, spared the hatred and greed and selfishness that is alive and well beyond our walls. You were born here, in a place that would accept you without reservation or judgment, and we were free to love you with our whole hearts. The world would have labeled your innocent life a sin, and considered you a pariah and an outcast. The nature of the problem that confronts you now is something beyond the scope of our understanding, so we have turned to the words of our Lord to find the answers you have required of us. There are two men at the crux of this dilemma, each equally dear to you. Each claim a share of your heart, and each one of them has given himself to you. The problem is you cannot belong to both of them, without betraying them, and yourself. You must make a choice between them, and the choice will cost you a part of your heart, no matter which way you decide."

Rita nodded, seeing that the Sisters had carved away all of the unimportant issues, and gotten to the very core of the matter. She looked at the faces of those who had been her earliest friends and companions. She waited for them to supply her with the final piece of the puzzle that would tip the balanced scale of her heart in one direction or the other.

"You made a decision to cross a bridge of friendship and enter into a different kind of relationship entirely. Your decision was not based on a desire for passion, but the nobler desire for compassion. The first man was your friend and your brother. He was at the center of your small world, and you felt safe and comfortable with him.

His feelings for you took another path, different than the one you were walking. You felt sorrow and guilt because of him. You did not share his feelings, and you wondered if you had done anything to mislead him. He was prepared to leave, so that you would not feel uncomfortable, or have a sense of obligation to him because of your strong bond. You yourself chose to cross the bridge to him, sacrificing something only you could give, and you could only offer it once. Then there is the matter of the second man. He is a good and honorable man, a healer who serves his fellow man unselfishly. You have known him for a far shorter time, but the backdrop of a war has intensified the flames of the horror you experience on a daily basis. You stand beside this man, and together the two of you fight to hold back death and loss. You feel empty and isolated as you are called on to attend to the pain and the suffering of these soldiers who have fallen in battle. You have now discovered a new path to explore; one that you never suspected could exist for you. This man has reached out for you, and you have crossed a bridge to be with him as well."

Rita bowed her head, listening to the Sister. The words crashing around inside her head made much less noise, when they were spoken by someone who loved you, and had the courage to tell you the truth.

"It is honorable to love, for whatever reason. You have made two commitments to two men, and now you must decide. Will you honor the first commitment you made, or will you honor the second commitment? The basis for deciding to act was different, and will have far reaching consequences for you all. You alone set your course, now you must choose. Will it be the first choice of compassion, or will you choose the second choice, passion? We can't help you there, we can only love you and pray for you and hope your choice will bring you peace and happiness." The mother Superior looked at Rita, wishing there was more that they could do, but they had spent all of their collected wisdom and experience on her behalf. The Sisters that crowded around her now, reaching out to touch her, and pass along their encouragement knowing they had done all they could. They hoped God would be able to complete what they had started, and Rita would understand what she must do.

They said their goodbyes with final hugs and tears. Rita made her way to the old door, knowing the world she had left behind a few hours ago was still out there waiting for her. She had come for comfort and clarity to this oasis in a storm. She now had a firm grasp of what she faced, without the confusion of reasons or excuses. It was simple now, but not easy. The Sisters were right, no matter which way she decided, it was going to cost her a piece of her heart. She pulled the door open, and walked out to face the world.

The German Sergeant saw her emerge from the Convent, and opened the door for her. Rita got inside, and headed back to her life, a life that was going to be experiencing some changes soon.

Chapter Nineteen

Rita went back to work with renewed vigor and energy. She kept her distance from Renato, and was professional but distant. He felt the change, but had no idea what had caused it. He too went forward with his work, extending Rita the courtesy of working out whatever was bothering her on her own terms. He was sad that they no longer were able to walk and talk together, and he desperately missed their closeness.

Rita would walk to her father's apartment alone now, spending her off hours in this tiny place of sanctuary. She had spent some of the happiest moments of her life there, as had her parents. She tried to draw from the aura of the familiar objects and the very walls of this place. Again and again she considered the things the mother Superior had said to her, condensing and burning away all of the secondary considerations. She knew she must choose; no one could do it for her. One cold raining evening, she grabbed her coat from the peg by the door and threw it over her head. She walked across the alley to Grandma Delia's home and knocked on the door.

"Oh, it is you my dear," answered the old woman, recognizing her under her makeshift umbrella. "Come in, you are all wet and shaking. Go over and stand by the fire and warm up before you catch your death. It has been such a long time since you have visited me. How have you been?"

Rita just hugged the woman who had become a grandmother to her. She couldn't think of anything to say, it was just good to be here with her. It hurt this dear woman to see Rita so down and defeated. How could the world crush such a beautiful flower, with so much love and tenderness in her heart? She decided to take advantage of their close friendship to break the ice, and say what was on her mind.

"My dear, I am an old woman, and I hope you will make allowances for me. I have lived too long to worry about my words, so I will be frank with you. I don't sleep too well, and the nights can be very long for me. It is my habit to look out my window, because there is nothing much that goes on inside my house of any interest. I have watched you bring home a young gentleman, and you must love him very much. I can imagine this is causing you a great deal of pain, because you don't want to disappoint those who live out at the Castle. You love them very much, and you feel a great strain for the expectations they have put on you. Am I right?" Grandma Delia looked at the shocked expression on Rita's face, knowing her secret was out. Before she could say anything, there was an unexpected knock on the door and Rita swung her head around in alarm.

"Oh dear Lord," whispered Rita, "it must be him! I can't speak to him now. Please tell him I went back to the Castle." Rita looked at her with pleading eyes, as she quickly stepped into the other room, and quietly shut the door.

Mrs. Delia followed her with her eyes, and then slowly made her way to the door. The young man standing in the rain on the other side of the door greeted her and said "Good evening Mrs. Delia. I am Dr. Renato Pini; I am a friend of Rita's from the hospital. She has mentioned you often, and I was hoping you might know where she is. I tried her father's apartment across the street, but there is no one there."

"She was here a little earlier, to pay me a visit. She said she was going to go home to the Castle tonight. She can't go home as often as she would like, and I am sure she misses her family. My daughter, Anna, is Rita's mother, you know." Mrs. Delia looked the young doctor in the eye, and kept her expression friendly and open. He thanked her for the information, and turned and disappeared into the rain.

"Thank you, I am sorry you had to lie for me," said Rita, coming out of the other room when she was sure he had gone.

"I spoke nothing but the truth! You did indeed visit me, it has been a long time since you have been home, and you said you were going out to the Castle," Grandma

Delia responded, with a distinct tone of indignation in her voice for being accused of telling a lie.

Rita hugged her, grateful for her support. "Thank God he is going home to Trento tomorrow, to visit his family. I will have some time to reflect on what I want to do." Rita was sad, with a sadness that filled her face.

"There is so much I would like to say to you, but I am afraid of over- stepping my bounds and speaking out of turn. I am an old lady now, and your generation is very different from the one I grew up in. I don't want to see you having to sneak down dark alleyways to find happiness. If you are to be happy, do so in the sunshine, and be proud of whom you wish to be happy with. If you have to make a sacrifice, do it now, before it will become more painful to everyone you love. That is the only way you will find any peace, and the blessings of God."

Chapter Twenty

God did indeed take a hand in Rita's life. After almost 4 years of war, the final push began with the Allied Forces crashing ashore in France. The Axis was driven steadily back, as they lost their grip on Europe on all fronts. The Fascists in Italy could no longer count on support from Germany, and the loyal Italian Partisans rallied to take back their beloved homeland from the maniacs who had almost destroyed it. As the American and English troops pushed their way up the boot of Italy, the German Army prepared to fall back to take up a defensive line around Germany itself.

Dr. Kruger and his German Staff were preparing to leave the hospital; they had been ordered to evacuate ahead of the advancing Allied Army. They would be leaving all of the equipment behind; there wasn't time or room to take it with them. Dr. Kruger wanted to say good bye to the people of the Castle that he had grown to love and respect. He had spent many pleasant evenings in their company, and they had helped him bear the separation from his family. He had become to think of them as family, and his concern for their well being was genuine. He had done a great deal for all of the people of Lake Braies, and had added immeasurably to the hospital. It was more than just the new wing and equipment; he had trained both the doctors and nurses who would be here continuing to serve the town, long after he had returned to Munich.

The shiny black Mercedes pulled up the gravel driveway for the last time, heading for the great fountain that now stood empty. The doctor got out of the car and looked around him at the still beautiful Estate. It was showing some wear from not having the people or supplies it required to perform at its best. He hoped the war would end soon, and the people who were such a part of this place would be able to love it back to life. He knew he would think of them often, as he prepared to return to his own home, to discover what might still remain there.

Dr. Kruger straightened his uniform, and looked down at his boots. This would not be a day for fine gray suits and enjoyable dining. He knocked at the door, and Count Donat opened it. He was invited inside, and courteously removed his hat.

"I have come to say good-bye, we will be leaving in a few hours, and I couldn't leave without saying 'thank you' for making me feel welcome. I have come to think of you as family, and I want to wish you the very best in the years to come." Dr Kruger stood in the foyer straight and tall, the image of a German officer.

"Thank you for coming to see us; you have been a refreshing surprise to us all. We didn't know when we saw your car come up the driveway the first time if it was a messenger of doom for our family. We were enemies during the First World War, and had some very firm prejudices established in our minds about Germans. Your courtesy and friendship have gone a long way to change our minds. It has been an honor to know you. Unfortunately you are still on the other side of a wide chasm that threatens to get wider every day. You have been very good to us in the time you have been in Lake Braies, and you will always be welcome here." Beppe extended his hand to a man that should have been an enemy, but had become a part of his family.

The doctor took his hand readily, with a firm grip that said he was sorry to be leaving. "We all have to do our duty. I am a doctor, and a German soldier. I have tried to make sure I served honorably in both of those callings. I will carry all of you home with me in my heart. You names will be spoken of with respect and love to all who know me."

"I owe you my thanks for looking after me, in spite of my own mule-headed stubbornness. I couldn't have had better medical attention if I lived in the hospital. The new prosthesis that you had designed for me is much more comfortable, and I can walk more like a man now, instead of a three legged dog." Guido, laughed, always the one who enjoyed his own jokes the most. He stepped forward and bypassed the doctor's hand, and favored him with his famous Alpini bear hug instead. It felt better to have a friend than an enemy.

"Thank you Sergeant," replied the doctor, aware of the great honor that had just been bestowed on him. "It was a privilege to take care of one of the Heroes of Italy. I shall miss your good humor, and the sound of your whistling."

"When you return home I hope you will make sure that Germany doesn't declare war on any of its neighbors any more. After two defeats it is time to just stay home and take care of your own country." Guido added, with a more serious note in his voice, from one soldier to another.

"That is my fervent hope as well, my friend," smiled the doctor sadly back at the people who had gathered to say good-bye. Donna Lucia stepped forward and hugged the doctor. He hugged her back and kissed her hand in farewell. Anna hugged him too, and gave him a kiss on the cheek. He had been so good to them, and had become a trusted and loyal friend. The doctor stepped back, and clicked his heels, with a last bow of respect, and headed down the stairs to the car.

His guard was standing at attention as he held the door open. He entered the car with a final wave, and then stepped inside and was gone. As the car turned off of the drive on to the main road, he heard a distant voice call his name. He turned to look in the direction they had come to see Rita, peddling her bicycle as fast as she could. He called for his driver to stop, and opened the door.

Rita closed the gap, and got off of her bike, out of breath from the exertion of catching up with the

Mercedes. "Dr. Kruger, I was afraid that I had missed you. I wanted to say thank you for all that you have done for my father. The new prosthetic leg that you made for him has made such a big difference in his life. He can get around in the gardens much easier, and working with the plants has always been his first love. I want to thank you for the opportunity to work on your staff at the hospital; I have learned so much in these few short years." Rita pulled out a small beautifully made wooden box from her pocket. "I wanted to give this to you to give to your daughters for me. This must have been a very sad time for them, and they must have missed you so much. I hope the music will remind them that you were with people who needed you, and we were grateful they shared you with us. Tell them I said that they have a very good father."

The doctor took the small inlaid box that Rita handed him, and opened it. It was a wind-up music box with a little ballerina inside. He knew his girls would be enchanted with the small treasure, and thanked Rita for her thoughtful gift. She gave him a hug good bye, as if she was sending off a favorite uncle on a long voyage. He hugged her back, and was surprised that he could still find tears, after all that he had seen.

"I will miss you and your family very much," admitted Kruger, with a smile, wiping his eyes. "You are an excellent nurse, one of the best I have ever worked with. I am sure there will plenty to keep you busy in the months to come. Perhaps we can drop you a card, from time to time, to stay in touch. Please continue with your education, but don't forget to have a little time for yourself as well." With one final hug, he got back into the interior of the big sedan, and headed for Lake Braies. The driver was anxious to be on their way, the reports of Allied troops closing in on their location were troubling, and he wanted to make sure he got the doctor away from there safely.

There was one final delay in leaving. He had to stop and say his farewells to the staff of the hospital that had been such a big part of his life. He made the rounds of the wards, one last time, pausing to shake hands and give last recommendations about treatments of patients still under his care. Among his interns and residents was Dr. Pini. He had particularly high praise for his talents and skills, as well as some words of advice of a personal nature.

"Dr Pini, I was just out to the Castle for one last visit. Count Donat and Guido Marron have become very dear to me, as have all of the members of their family. They have treated me like a member of their family, and have helped me with homesickness when I was missing my own wife and daughters in Munich. Count Donat's son, Paul, has been away at medical school in Geneva, and I expect that he will be returning soon after the war has wound down. This is a very close family, and I know that Beppe and Guido share a cherished dream that their children would marry, upon Paul's return. Rita and Paul have grown up together, and it would be a good start to helping recover from all that this war has cost them. I do not mean to delve into your private life, but I would hope that you would think about what I have said, as you think about your plans for the future." Kruger extended his hand to his young colleague, and prepared to leave.

Renato took his proffered hand, and shook it warmly, grateful for all that the other doctor had taught him. "I do hope that you will arrive home safely, Dr. Kruger, and thank you for all you have taught me. I couldn't have had a better teacher, or a better example of what a doctor should be." He looked at the soldier/doctor with the big heart, with respect and regret. He had introduced Rita to him, and he had given him some sound advice that he hoped he had the courage to follow. Dr Kruger was a great human being, and it gave him hope that people could learn to work together, despite their differences, in the years ahead. It would require the good will of people from all over the world to rebuild their battered countries and shattered lives.

Chapter Twenty-one

In Switzerland, they took the news of the end of the war with the same joy felt all around the world. They had been spared the fighting and destruction, but they had still lived on the edge between all of the combatants. Paul and Philip were preparing to take their final exams before receiving their doctorate degrees in neurology and psychiatry. It felt like they had spent a life time here, studying and working. Paul had mixed feelings as his time in this beautiful country was coming to a close. He loved being here with his aunt and uncle, and Philip had become the brother he missed having. Their love and moral support and financial support had meant the world to him, with no word from Lake Braies getting through. He loved Geneva, with its big wide streets full of people, and the shops that crowded every building. He loved the University, and felt so fortunate to have received his education here. He would take the things that he had been taught home to Lake Braies with him, to help his people recover from the war they had met head on. The person most on his mind had always been Rita. Their parting had been unexpectedly intimate, but with much left unsettled between them. He knew she still had doubts in her mind, and he was both eager and nervous to see her again. What would her eyes say to him, when they saw each other after so long?

Philip and Lena Muller were very much in love, and they tried to see each other when they could. Paul tried to stay busy when Lena was in town, to avoid the temptation of Janet. He couldn't deny that there was something there, with the time they had spent together during her recovery. It was disturbingly easy to forget the girl that might be waiting for him at home, when he was faced with Janet's beauty and charm. Janet Muller, for her part, was quite taken with the handsome young Italian doctor who had saved her life. She knew that Paul's heart seemed to be somewhere else, but she didn't care. She would be grateful for any crumb of his affection that he would throw her; the future didn't matter to her, she just wanted him.

Paul and Janet happened to run into each other, when she had accompanied Lena to Geneva to visit Philip. It had been a very long time since Paul and Rita had said their goodbyes, and Paul to his eternal shame yielded to temptation. It would be so easy for him to stay here and be with Janet for the rest of his life. She was wonderful, and he could feel himself falling in love with her. He hated himself for being so weak, and thought about those that would be so disappointed in him back at home. He was their hope for the future. They had sacrificed for him and had remained home in Italy, to care for the Estate. He couldn't even dare to think about what they were enduring while he was safe here in Switzerland. He truly hated himself, and felt completely unworthy of their love and support. He would go home to Lake Braies, and do the things that were expected of him.

Back in Lake Braies, a similar scene was unfolding. Dr. Renato Pini was doing the best he could to follow the advice of his mentor, and stay away from Rita. It was difficult for Rita too, since she worked with Renato, and saw him on a daily basis. It was driving a stake through her heart to see the man she loved, to hear his voice, and to know she must never touch him again. She was forced to live in a cage with an open door. The strong sense of duty, honor, and obligation to her family and to Paul, was the jailer that held the key to Rita's happiness.

Rita was able to spend more time at home, now that the war was over and the influx of new casualties had dried up. There were still many soldiers recovering from their injuries at the hospital, but the endless lines of trucks that made their way to the emergency entrance of the hospital had abated. It felt good to spend more time with her family, and to feel the normal routine of their old life start to fall into place. Guido was delighted to have Rita home more, but the person who noticed the hidden sadness in Rita's eyes was Anna.

"I have watched you since the war ended, and you have been able to come home to us. At first I thought it was because of all of the terrible things that you have seen as a nurse at the hospital. Now I am not so sure. Can you tell me what is troubling you? We have always been close, and I was grateful that you thought of me as your mother. I am here for you, and I will listen if you want to talk." Anna's eyes were gentle, as she looked back at Rita, pleading for her to let her in.

Rita was grateful for Anna's insight and caring nature. She fell into her mother's arms, and released the burden she had been carrying for too long. Like the morning that Paul had left for Switzerland, Anna just held Rita in her arms, and rocked her and listened. When Rita had finally cried herself out, Anna tried to find words to comfort her.

"You must not worry, my love, things will work themselves out, they always do. Paul will return from Geneva one of these days, and then we will see what is to be done." Anna continued to rock Rita in her arms, and prayed to a loving God to ease her troubled mind and heal her wounded soul.

Chapter Twenty-two

It was the occasion of Saint Joseph's Day in Lake Braies, and the whole town was celebrating. Count Donat was named after Saint Joseph, so there was always a party at the Castle as well. The extra food that the good Dr. Kruger had supplied to them during the war was almost gone, but the Estate was starting to produce a few things of its own again. They didn't mind the light meals so much; they all had enough to fill their stomachs, even if the variety wasn't the best. There was peace at last, and they were excited about planning for the farms and gardens again. Before they knew it, there would be a surplus to send to the market faire in town, just like they did before the war. Anna brought a cake, with real frosting on it, in from the kitchen. It had been a long time since the kitchen had produced a cake, and everyone was looking forward to it. The bell for the front door rang, and faithful Nina went to answer it. She was the only one of the servants that had been able to remain in the service of the Donats. She required very little to make her happy, and this was her home. It didn't matter that they couldn't pay her anything; she would always love them and serve them.

When she opened the front door, the light of the sunshine beaming in to the darken hall temporarily blinded her. She squinted to make out the form of the man standing on the steps and she heard, "Hello Nina, don't you recognize me?" With that he swooped in and scooped the tiny woman into his arms, hugging her to his chest.

"Mr. Paul, is that really you?" Nina let out a laugh of pure happiness, as he swung her around. The rest of the family seated in the dining room heard her laughter, and came running to investigate the cause. They all headed for the front door, and their cries of delight and laughter were added to Nina's as they recognized who was standing there. They all rushed for him, everyone's arms overlapping, as they all tried to hug him at the same time. Rita hung back a little, not knowing if she had the right to welcome him home. It took a moment for everyone to settle down, and gain their composure. As Rita looked at him, the years that he had been gone melted away, and her best friend was standing there again. She finally rushed forward and grabbed him, forgetting the dread and fear she thought might cloud his arrival. This was Paul, her brother, her best friend. He was home, and Anna was right, everything would work itself out, this was all that mattered for now. They were alive, and the family was whole again.

Paul was overwhelmed to have Rita back in his arms again. He had forgotten how beautiful she was. The time he had been away from her was suddenly just a fleeting moment, and the last four years a dream that was fading away as he woke up. He was home, and the people he loved were here and safe. He had worried so much about them, always wondering if they were alive, if the Castle was still here. He could see that the war had been very hard on them, and he cringed inside. They all looked thin and there was an air of weariness to the lines in their faces. Their clothes were clean and mended, but before the war they wouldn't have bothered to give clothes in this condition to the local charity. Again he felt guilt for the life of ease and plenty he had enjoyed in the Palace of his aunt and uncle. He resolved that he would work very hard to repay them all for their sacrifice. He had no doubt if he had been home he would have found himself in the army. Paul did not have to be told how many families were weeping for the men who would never return.

The Donats had always served their country, when the call to duty came. He would have to serve now in helping his family and his town to recover from the war which he had been spared.

"I am home, now," Paul spoke with the confidence born of conviction. "We will rebuild our home and our lives better than they were before this war. We are a strong family, and together we will forge a future of our choosing."

"I am so glad to have you home again, my son," beamed Beppe. "There were times that I doubted that would ever happen. It is fitting that you have returned on Saint Joseph's Day, your safe return to us is God's assurance that everything will be good again." There were as many tears streaming down Beppe's face, as there were on Donna Lucia's face. She had not found the strength to release Paul's hand.

"This is indeed the best celebration we have ever had!" laughed Guido, still trying to make himself believe that Paul was really home at last. "Why are we all standing out here in the foyer when there is a cake that is crying out for company in the dining room?" They all laughed, and nodded, and headed in the direction of dessert.

Rita now had both of her loves in Lake Braies, her brother and her faithful doctor. She has had all of the advice that she needed; now it was all up to her. She would be patient and wait for that answer that she knew that God would eventually send her. Her trip to the convent taught her that faith, patience, and courage will bring her anything she desires, if her requests are in keeping with God's will.

Paul was happy to be home, too, and he was facing a similar choice. He was desperately needed here at home, and he still loved Rita more than his own life. He felt guilty for betraying her, and wondered what kind of a man he was, loving one woman, and letting another woman distract him. How strong could his love be? His father would have never betrayed his mother in this manner. He was eaten up with shame, but it was a silent shame he felt he must bear alone. He couldn't talk to his father or his uncle Guido about his doubts and fears; they would be crushed to learn that he had been so weak and faithless.

As the weather got warmer, Rita and Paul resumed their nightly walks. The garden that they both loved was in a sad state of repair compared to the splendor they once knew. Still, it was a familiar place to be together and renew their old bonds. They talked about the years they spent apart, and the events of their lives. There was school and classes to discuss, and the hospitals they both worked in. Rita talked of the causalities, and the endless rounds of surgeries that filled her days. There were all the changes at the hospital in Lake Braies, and the tall German officer that was responsible for them. They talked of the slow friendship that emerged between the two old Alpini and a man who should have been their enemy. His care of Guido's leg and the new leg that helped him get around in the garden so much better. His kindness to Rita in getting her the best training available, and the regular deliveries of food to the Castle, when there were few people to work the Estate. Paul talked of his life with his family in Geneva and the strong bond he developed with his cousin, Philip. He spoke of their work in neurology, and the sleepless nights as an intern. He talked of his graduation from Medical School, and how it felt to graduate at the top of his class.

They both covered every milestone in their lives, except the two that they would each have found so helpful. Those were private burdens that each of them had decided was their responsibility to bear in silence. If they were never spoken of, then they never existed.

When Paul toured the hospital, with its new wing and improvements and the expanded staff, he was impressed by what he saw. He would have enjoyed the opportunity to meet this Dr. Kruger that he had heard so much about. It was apparent by the care and the eye for detail that he had taken that he was a man who prided himself on doing a good job. Paul was especially impressed by the respect that was shown to Rita, both as a nurse and as a person. It was clear that she was very important to everyone here, and the best at what she did. The hospital was bigger and better than it was before he had left for Switzerland. One of the few good things to emerge from the war was a hospital that would now be able to serve the people of Lake Braies, and the surrounding region, making it unnecessary to travel to Trento any longer.

Like all hospitals, news travels fast. It was on everyone's lips that Paul Donat had returned from Switzerland. He had graduated at the top of his class, and he had two degrees, one in neurology and one in psychiatry. Neither of these specialties was available at the hospital, and there would be new programs opening to train the staff. As they walked the halls of the hospital,

Rita introduced Paul to the doctors and nurses that were new to him.

It was inevitable that they would eventually run into Dr. Renato Pini, and Rita made the introductions. He was a highly respected surgeon, and he had worked on Dr. Kruger's personal staff. He and Rita had worked together frequently, and Paul thought it odd that Rita seemed rather cold and distant to him. He just dismissed it; sometimes there were people you just didn't hit it off with.

"I am happy to meet you Dr. Donat, the hospital has been talking about nothing but you since your return. The University in Geneva is an excellent school, and there is a great need for both of your specialties here. You must be glad to be home with your family. My own family is in Trento, so I don't get to see them as often as I would like. You are a lucky man to have a fiancé like Rita, she is a good nurse and everyone likes her." Renato gave him a good handshake, and an easy smile.

"Thank you Dr. Pini, you are right—it is good to be home. I am very impressed with all of the improvements to the hospital since I've been gone. I understand that you graduated from the University in Milan. That is also a highly respected teaching school. I look forward to working with you, and sharing our training together." Paul smiled back at him, this was a good man, "You are also right about Rita, we grew up together, and have always been the best of friends. We are still getting to know each other again, after such a long absence, but our families are hoping that they will get to plan a wedding one of these days."

Rita coughed, and the tears came to her eyes as she tried to catch her breath. She finally coughed again, and the gum she had been chewing fell out of her mouth on the floor. She laughed and picked up the gum in a piece of paper, and put it in the trash. "I guess it is true what they say," laughed Rita with an easy grace she didn't feel, "some people can't walk and chew gum at the same time! I will have to be more careful, next time I could cough up a lung." They all enjoyed a good laugh. Renato returned to his patients. Paul and Rita continued their tour of the ward. Rita resumed her commentary on Dr. Kruger's methods and improvements.

Chapter Twenty-three

All of Italy was ready to wake up from the long nightmare that had been the Second World War. Everywhere there were signs of recovery, as help streamed in from all over the world. The Americans were at the vanguard, as they had been during the last war. Many of them were returning servicemen who had served in Italy, fallen in love, and married Italian women. There was a hunger for more than just the shipments of food that were sent in great quantities. People wanted to hear music and laughter and see plays and enjoy the culture that was their homeland. There were weddings everywhere, as servicemen returned home. There had been too much death and sorrow; it was time to think about the future and raising families.

In Lake Braies, a town surrounded by some of the finest skiing in the region, they were looking forward to the first snow fall of the season. It would be good to see the tourists return, as they had for longer than anyone could remember. At the Castle on the other side of the lake, the Estate was slowly gathering its strength. There were a few more people around to help out now, but money was still in scarce supply. It was not uncommon to trade work and services for food and supplies. The monetary system of Italy was still reeling from the cost of the war. People were happy to have enough to eat, and a roof over their head, in exchange for useful work. The Donats had always been good to the people who had worked on the Estate and a few of the same people had come back to them after the war.

Rita and Paul kept trying to renew their friendship, but there seemed to be something that stood between them and the way they should have felt. They still loved each other with all of their hearts, and enjoyed being together, but it didn't feel like the giddy love that should be attending two people who were planning to spend the rest of their lives together. Still, there was the expectation of their families, and they wanted very much to make them happy. Was it such an unreasonable request, considering all that they had been through together? There was such misery and grief every where they turned, a marriage between two best friends seemed like a good thing, so the plans went forward.

The picturesque little Chapel where the family had attended church together for centuries was the site of their wedding. The beautiful red carpet had been carefully cleaned, and the gardens had provided a bounty of beautiful flowers to adorn the simple altar. Rita was a vision in the antique white wedding dress that had belonged to Paul's Grandmother, Donna Hermenia. Rita had been a particular favorite of hers, when she had come to live at the Castle. Rita felt the sweet presence of that noble woman near, as she slipped on the dress that had waited so patiently in the beautiful old cedar chest. The lovely lace veil that covered her face seemed a little out of place with her wistful expression. Rita was happy enough, she thought, but she couldn't help but think that this should be the happiest day of her life.

She looked at her father, standing next to her, in his freshly cleaned and pressed suit. She seldom saw him in a suit, preferring instead his favorite old clothes that he worked in the gardens. He looked so happy, as if he were thinking about his own marriage to Anna in this very chapel. Perhaps he was dreaming what it would have been like to see his beloved Maria walking towards him in a vision of white and carrying a bouquet that he had made for her himself. He had made so many bridal bouquets over the year, as had his father. He was proud that he had raised the flowers for the bouquet that he had brought to her early this morning. Anna and Donna Lucia had each given her something for her ensemble, a beautiful comb for her hair, and a lovely blue necklace.

Paul had his own thoughts as he dressed for the wedding. His mother was so excited when she brought him her Grandfather's beautiful tie clasp. It had been necessary to sell much of the family's heirlooms in order to help the Estate survive, but there were still some special pieces that they would never part with. She chatted happily as she helped him put his tie on, and get it adjusted just right. Then she put the tie clasp in place, and stood back to admire it. There were tears in her eyes, as she looked at her son with pride. He was the spitting image of his great grandfather, and it pleased her so to see him wearing the clasp. She hugged him, and hurried off, with half a hundred things still to do before she was done.

Beppe knocked and entered Paul's room to see if he needed any help. He was so excited that Rita and Paul had decided to get married. He and Guido had talked of nothing else, since the two of them had made the announcement at dinner one night. He was talking about when he and Lucia had gotten married in the very same Chapel. He was so nervous that he kept stumbling over his wedding vows. The priest had to hide his face behind his prayer book to keep from laughing out loud. He talked about Guido and Anna's wedding, and how happy they looked. He wanted to know if Paul needed any "advice" about their wedding night, and Beppe seemed very relieved when Paul just laughed and assured him that he didn't. Since Paul didn't have any close friends currently living in Lake Braies, Beppe was going to stand up with him as his best man. Beppe had suggested Paul invite Philip to be his best man. Donna Lucia hadn't seen her sister and her brother-in-law since before the war. Paul was quick to turn down that idea; he didn't want Philip to accidentally mention Janet, as he was sure to bring up her sister Lena. He knew his father and Uncle Guido would be quick to put all of the pieces together, and that was the last thing that he wanted. He had strayed, but he never meant for anyone to learn about his indiscretion. It was better if Philip remained in Switzerland.

The wedding was a small affair, just family and a few close friends from Lake Braies and the hospital. One person who was not there from the hospital was Dr. Pini. He was away on vacation visiting his family in Trento. Guido walked Rita down the aisle, and handed her over to Paul. The vows were simple, and no one objected to their union, although both Paul and Rita probably should have. They decided to bury their feelings, and make their families happy.

Chapter Twenty-four

They took a short honeymoon in the mountains of Cortina D' Ampezzo, in the northern part of Italy. The scenery was breathtaking, and they enjoyed being together, but they both were thinking of someone else on their wedding night. They were friends, and they got along well together, but there was no real fire between them. They went back to Lake Braies, and took up residence in the Castle. It was so large that they had a whole wing to themselves, so there was privacy. Paul joined the staff of the hospital, and started up a training program for neurology and psychiatry. He was very busy, and put in very long hours at the hospital. Rita was equally busy at the hospital with her nursing. She was careful to try and work in an area of the hospital where she wouldn't run into Renato if she could help it. She accepted additional hours at the hospital by teaching in the nursing program. She and Paul would drive to work in the morning, and perhaps they would have lunch together, if their schedules allowed it. They would drive home together, and they would both be exhausted by the end of their day. They were comfortable together, but it was the comfort of a brother and sister, or two roommates. They would walk together in the garden, and talked about their work at the hospital. The days seemed to pass, and they were content, but neither could help but think about a greater happiness that they might have had.

Paul and Rita were married two years, when Rita announced that she was expecting a baby. Beppe and Guido were on top of the world, and Donna Lucia and Anna were busy getting things put together for the baby's room. They made many trips to the storage area in the upper rooms of the Castle. It had been many years since the crib and baby furniture were needed. The beautiful handmade crib was at least two hundred years old, and had held several generations of Donats. It was like a breath of life in the Castle to contemplate the sound of little feet scampering up and down the hallways.

It was a difficult pregnancy, and Rita had to stop working after her fifth month and rest. It was important to stay off her feet as much as she could, to prevent any premature labor. Rita and Paul were both looking forward to the birth of their first child. If their marriage was a marriage of convenience, like arranged marriages among the nobility of the past, their pride and excitement as they anticipated the arrival of their first born was genuine.

The days passed slowly for Rita; she loved being at the hospital, but she realized she needed to do all that she could to insure the baby was safe. She enjoyed sitting outside in the garden near her father as he worked. He would set up cushions on one of the comfortable chairs near where he was working, and Rita would sit and enjoy his company. Anna and Donna Lucia frequently joined them, while they worked on little things for the baby. Anna was an expert with a pair of knitting needles, and was turning out socks and hats and sweaters for their new little arrival. Donna Lucia liked to crochet, and had made several nice blankets. Beppe would join the group, bringing lunch down from the Castle. While everyone enjoyed the latest wine from the vineyard, there was always a pitcher of milk for Rita.

Paul was spending less time at the hospital than before Rita's pregnancy. He would find himself looking at the clock frequently, so he could go home and be with Rita and the rest of the family. They were all so happy. It seemed like they were finally turning a new page, and the war was slowly fading away. Paul worked in his own wing of the hospital, and seldom had occasion to see or work with Dr. Pini. On the few times that they did work together, he thought it was odd that Dr. Pini seemed to be unaware of the attention that some of the nurses in the hospital paid to him. He was a very serious-minded doctor, and he didn't seem to notice anything but his patients and his students. Paul would catch a nurse watching Dr. Pini, or make an obvious overture towards him, but he just didn't seem to notice, or care, as far as Paul could tell.

Rita was sitting outside, enjoying the sunshine, visiting with Anna and Donna Lucia. It was a beautiful day, and the birds were intent on outdoing each other with their new songs. Rita was resting more and more, and she was experiencing pains in her back. It was getting more difficult to walk; she joked that she looked more like the ducks down at the lake, when they waddled up on the banks. Paul was sitting on the end of the outdoor couch with Rita, rubbing her feet. In the last few weeks she had been experiencing some swelling, and it felt good to have him rub them after she had been up for a while. Guido and Beppe were down at the livestock pens, checking on several cows that were due soon. As Rita shifted her weight to try to get into a little more comfortable position, she suddenly felt very odd. The next thing she knew it felt like something had dropped and she could hear the sound of moisture hitting the gravel under the wicker couch.

Paul looked at her in alarm, and she just started laughing. "It looks like the storks will be bringing more than calves to the Estate today," giggled Rita. "I thought I just had a sore back this morning when I woke up, now it looks like I was actually starting the first rounds of labor pains."

Donna Lucia and Anna jumped to their feet and rushed over to Rita. Paul gently set her feet down. "I think it is time we took you over to the hospital," smiled Paul, "You have been lying around the house too much lately; it is time you showed up for your shift and did some real labor!" Rita laughed at his play on words, and then the first serious labor pain hit her, and changed her mind about laughing. She held her side, and breathed with the pain, until it let up, nodding that she was all right.

"I think you are right, Paul, I don't want to be late for work!" He reached down and helped Rita get to her feet. "Momma, would you go and get the bag I have packed in my room by the door? Mother, would you go and tell Uncle Beppe and father that they are about to become grandfathers? I would appreciate your assistance getting to the car, Paul, my balance wasn't much before, but now I am dripping all over the place." Paul just nodded, and held her tightly with one hand, and kept his arm around her shoulder with the other.

"I have seen quite a few babies delivered in the past, but when it is your own wife going into labor, and your first child getting ready to make his appearance, it is very different somehow. I want to do everything at once, and I can't seem to figure out what order I should do them in! Let's sit you down here for a minute, Rita, while I go bring the car up. It would be better if you didn't have to walk too far." Paul gently lowered Rita into a chair with arms, so it would be easier for her to get up again, and headed off at a dead run to get the car. Donna Lucia had found Beppe and Guido, and they came back to the veranda as fast as they could. Both of the men could use a shower, and a clean set of clothes, but there was no time for that. Anna showed up with Rita's bag, just as Paul appeared around the corner of the Castle with the car.

They loaded Rita into the back seat of the car, with a big towel for her to sit on, and headed for the hospital.

When the car showed up at the emergency entrance, the staff recognized who it was and everyone swung into high gear. They got Rita a wheelchair, and headed off to the delivery room, with most of those on duty trailing after them. Guido, Beppe, Anna, and Donna Lucia all went to the waiting area and tried to sit, but it was difficult. Beppe would get up and walk back and forth, and then Guido would. Since Paul was a doctor at the hospital, he had every intention to be there when his child arrived. Most fathers would just be sitting in the waiting room, pacing with the rest of the family.

First babies usually take longer arriving, and Paul and Rita's baby was no exception. Paul stayed right there by Rita's side, since pediatrics wasn't his specialty. It was hard for him to see her in pain, and the prolonged labor was taking a toll on her strength. All he could do was wipe her forehead, and hold her hand and encourage her. Every once in a while a very strong labor pain would hit Rita, and she would bear down so hard on his hand it felt like she would break it. He could only imagine what she was going through.

After long weary hours, and one final Herculean last push, the newest member of the Donat family decided it was time to say hello. It was a strong healthy baby boy, and he let everyone in the room know he was not too happy about the chilly room or the bright lights. After the smiling nurses cleaned him, and weighed and measured him, they wrapped him up, and handed him to an exhausted but smiling Rita. Paul was sitting beside her on the bed with his arm around her, and he just stared with awe and amazement at their new son. He had seen some beautiful babies before, but he was certain that there had never been a baby as beautiful as this one.

As the new family sat there together, getting acquainted, it felt like the world was finally starting to make sense again. Paul kissed Rita on the forehead, and beamed at her. Rita smiled back, grateful that she had been patient and waited for God's confirmation on the course of her life. She couldn't imagine being more happy than she was at this moment. She thought about her mother, as she had held her for a few minutes before she had to leave her forever. She understood what her mother had felt, and indeed, all of her mothers at the convent. She could imagine them holding her, when she was just a few minutes old, passing her from hand to hand. It was easy to understand how they could love her so easily, and why they all doted on her even now.

"He is amazing. I can understand what my father must have felt like, when he saw me for the first time. I just want to hold him, and protect him, and never let anything hurt him, ever. Speaking about fathers, I guess I better go tell them the good news. I'll bet they have all worn a hole in the carpet by now!" Rita looked up at Paul and laughed. She was sure that there would be a race down the hall to see who could get here first. Paul bent down and kissed his son before he left, hating to go, but knowing if he didn't he would be in for a real tongue-lashing from four very cross grandparents.

Paul stuck his head in the waiting room, looking to see how the grandparents had held up under the strain. Beppe was looking out the window, as the sun was making its appearance over the mountains. Guido was sitting on the couch, rubbing his leg. Paul could easily imagine that Guido had been on his feet all night, matching Beppe step for step. Anna and Donna Lucia were sitting on the other side of the room, discussing things that grandmothers talked about together. Donna Lucia was the first to spy Paul sticking his head in the door, and rose quickly to her feet, followed closely by Anna. Beppe heard her draw in a quick breath of surprise and anticipation, and turned around to see Paul's smiling face. Guido was the first to find his voice, and called out, "I never took you for a sadistic man, Paul Donat! Tell us already, what do we have?"

Paul just laughed and shook his head, that was so like Uncle Guido.

"We have a fine healthy baby boy. He was born a few minutes ago. Rita is tired, but she is fine. He has black hair, and it was hard to tell, but I think his eyes are green like Rita's. I have seen quite a few babies, since I became a doctor, but I think this is the most beautiful one I have ever seen. I don't suppose that you would like to take a look at him, and tell me if you agree?"

With that, they all made for the door, and almost bowled the new father over. Father's were all right, but it was the grandparents that were the true center of a child's life. Most people had to see their new grandbaby from the other side of a cold clinical pane of glass, but these grandparents had a lot of pull in this hospital. Anna was the first to stick her head in, and Rita looked up at her and motioned her to come in, all of them to come in. Rita handed the new love of her life to his father, and tried to sit up a little better in the bed. The family gathered around Paul, and gazed adoringly at the most beautiful baby in the world. They all agreed, Paul was being far too modest and skimpy with his praise, when he had described him.

Anna was the first to get the honor to hold him, but Lucia was so close at her side the two women could have been Siamese Twins. Anna handed the baby to Lucia, and Lucia held him like a priceless piece of porcelain. "He looks very much like your papa, Beppe," Lucia said, smiling at her husband. She could see that Beppe agreed with her because there were tears in his eyes. Guido was overcome with the moment, and had a similar problem with his own eyes. They both let their wives hold him as long as they wanted, well, as long as they could stand not having a turn of their own.

Paul went back over to sit beside Rita, as they watched their normally reasonable parents dissolve into doting grandparents that would spoil this poor baby until he was rotten. They were all making little noises and kissing sounds with their lips. Babies couldn't see too well when they were first born, but this mob didn't care, and were fully engaged in what appeared to be an elaborate game of charades.

Beppe looked up at his own son, as Lucia finally allowed him to hold his Grandson for the first time. "Have the two of you decided on a name? I know you have talked about quite a few, but somehow Anna Lucia Donat doesn't seem to suit him!" Beppe laughed, but was careful not to enjoy his own joke too loudly.

"We tried out a lot of combinations over the last few weeks, but we finally decided that he should be named after all of the fine Alpini in our family. Rita and I like the sound of Francesco Giuseppe Guido Donat." Paul smiled at his father and his uncle, as they tried out the name between them, mouthing the words silently. They were smiling at little Francesco, and pronouncing his name slowly out loud so he could decide if he like it or not. He gave a loud burp in reply, so they all agreed it was the sign that he thought it was a fine name. The nurse taking care of Rita and little Francesco decided they had crowded the hospital rules long enough, and it was time for her two charges to get some rest, as they had both had a busy day. The family nodded in reluctant agreement, and after last kisses and gentle touches, allowed themselves to be herded out the door. Paul decided to sleep in the chair in Rita's room; he would have to be on duty in a few hours anyway. He couldn't bring himself to leave them, just yet.

The two of them were finally feeling the happiness they had been missing. They could now lavish on their son, the kind of love they didn't seem to generate from their own relationship. There was kindness and courtesy and genuine fondness, but it was less than they could have hoped for. Now they felt complete, and the future looked like a better place.

Chapter Twenty-five

When things are going well, and there is happiness in abundance, it always seems to attract the brooding dark clouds that live somewhere just over the horizon. Beppe began to experience headaches. At first they were mild and infrequent. He would take some medicine, and be fine. The headaches slowly began to be more frequent, and were not as easily persuaded to go away. They were all sitting in the dining room, having dinner together one evening, when Paul noticed that his father was rubbing the side of his head.

"Do you have a headache, Papa?" Paul looked at Beppe; it was seldom that his father didn't feel well.

"Oh, you know, it comes and goes. I used to have headaches when I was in Trento, after the war. I got a pretty good smack on the head from an incoming shell, but it went away after I came home to Lake Braies. Here lately, I seem to be having some headaches again, once in a while. Perhaps the war isn't through with me yet." Beppe laughed, trying to put his family at ease, and not worry them.

"You don't have to worry about that, Alpino, there isn't enough metal in a shell to keep you down," Guido declared, trying to hide the concern he was really feeling for his brother.

"Just the same, I would feel better if we had a look at it in the morning at the hospital. After all, headaches are one of my specialties, so I would appreciate your business! We will take an x-ray of your hard head tomorrow, and see what is ailing you. I will go get you something from my bag to take care of the headache—you will be feeling better soon," smiled Paul, but he felt a little uneasy.

"That's good; I wouldn't want anything to keep me from enjoying the best grappa we have produced from our vineyard since before the war." Beppe, poured out the new bottle, and took a moment to look around the table at everyone he loved the most in this world.

The next morning Beppe and Guido went with Paul to the hospital.

Rita was worried about Beppe, but she was busy with the baby. Anna, Donna Lucia, and Nina were always there to help her. Rita felt certain that Francesco would probably be in grade school before he learned to walk. None of his adoring family ever allowed his feet to touch the ground, so the poor child had no idea what they were for. They just waited at home for word on Beppe's results.

Paul held the x-ray up to the light, and squinted at a faint dark shadow on the right side of the film. He looked at several other angles, to make sure it wasn't a flaw on the film. It was small, a sliver of an image, but after double-checking, he was sure there was something there. He called the hospital in Trento, and requested the x-rays that had been taken when Beppe had been treated there for his head wound.

Things were rather chaotic in those days, and a lot of medical files and diagnostic material had been misplaced or gone missing. They promised to try and find them, but they weren't optimistic.

Paul decided to send copies of his father's x-ray to his old Professor in Geneva, Dr. Max Muller. Paul thought he knew what was causing his father's symptoms, but he wanted a second opinion. If the image in the x-ray was indeed a shell fragment left behind when they treated his wound, it had been there a very long time. It was very deep, and in a part of his brain that would be difficult and dangerous to try and retrieve.

He knew that his father would want him to tell him the truth; he would be disappointed in Paul if he tried to keep anything from him. He showed both Beppe and Guido the x-ray, and pointed out the small dark shadow. He told them that he had called his old teacher in Geneva, and he was sending it to him for a second opinion. The two of them would talk when Dr. Muller had the x-ray, and decide what to do then. In the meantime Paul didn't see any reason for Beppe to stay in the hospital. He wrote out a prescription for his father, and Guido and Beppe took the car and went back to the Castle.

In the days that followed, while they waited for Dr. Muller to receive Beppe's x-rays, everyone at the Castle did what they could to keep him in good spirits. Guido especially spent extra time with his friend and brother to reassure him. They played cards together, and laughed and remembered and drank Grappa together. Rita made sure that Beppe spent as much time with Francesco as possible. The little boy loved Beppe, and squealed with delight when his grandfather would play with him. The two of them loved to explore the garden together, and Francesco would bring him small treasures of pretty pebbles and flowers crushed in his tiny fist. Anna, Lucia, and Nina could be seen, at various times of the day making their way to the chapel, on some imagined errand or other. They went to pray for Beppe's recovery, and plead with God to allow them the blessing of his company for many more years. Paul spent more time at home, so that he would be with his father, and monitor his condition, without being too obvious about it. They all ate together and enjoyed life to the fullest, but there was always the specter of doubt and fear prowling around the boarders of their happiness.

The call Paul had been waiting for finally came one afternoon, as he sat at his desk taking care of a pile of paperwork that needed to be cleaned up. He jumped when the phone rang, and stared at it for a moment, knowing it would be Dr. Muller. "Hello, Dr. Donat, this is Dr. Muller returning your call. Your father's x-rays arrived here in the morning's mail, and I have been going over them and reviewing them with the rest of my staff. We all agree that it is most certainly a small shell fragment from the injury your father suffered during the war. It is amazing that it has remained there so long, without any consequences until now. I have talked to a number of my colleagues, and I am afraid that we are all in agreement. If the fragment remains, his condition will continue to deteriorate, and he will be in increasing pain. At some point he will lapse into a coma and eventually die. There is the option of surgery to remove the fragment, but the location is extremely deep, and in a very delicate area of his brain. The surgery is very risky, and could cause blindness or cognitive impairment. The most serious consequence, of course would be death. I wish I had better news for you, but we are men of Medicine, and it is of no constructive purpose to be less than truthful."

"I concur, Dr. Muller," added Paul; glad that he at least had the information he had been waiting for. "What are your recommendations?"

"This is a very difficult case. Neither of the options is very attractive, and both could have the same results. That is something that your father and your family are going to have to decide, because you are the ones who will live with the decision. I am most grateful for what you and Dr Von Strass did for my family, when we faced our greatest hour of need. If you decide to operate, I will come to Lake Braies and assist you with the surgery. Between the two of us I believe we can insure the best outcome possible for your father. If you decide to go ahead with the surgery, I would advise that we do it sooner, rather than later, to increase our chances of having a successful operation. I will take steps to begin to rearrange my schedule, and have other doctors here at the University cover my classes and my patients. I will be ready when you call, and I can be on a train in a matter of hours. I do not envy you the task ahead; it is hard to know which one is the best course of action. I will alert my staff to reach me, no matter where I am when you call. Good luck, Doctor. We will be praying for you."

"Thank-you, Dr. Muller, I will speak to my father and my family tonight. He will appreciate you candor and your offer of assistance. I will let you know what we decide. Ultimately the decision will rest with him," With that, Paul hung up the phone and sat for a moment, wondering if he should go home early and let them know what Dr. Muller said. He decided that his father would not approve of him neglecting his other duties to be a messenger boy, so he finished all of his work before knocking off for the night.

At dinner that evening, after the plates were cleared away, and his father poured the grappa, he relayed the information from Dr. Muller's call. There was silence as he covered all of the things that his old teacher had covered with him. Paul was open about the options and the consequences, along with his mentor's offer to come to Lake Braies and assist with the surgery. Beppe listened carefully, and asked a few questions when Paul was done.

"You have given us a great deal to think about," commented Beppe, as he looked around the table at his family. He could see the worry in their eyes, as they grasped the reality that he could die, either way they decided. "We will take a few days to talk, and we will ask the Good Lord's opinion, too.

"I am glad that you have spoken so openly tonight, it is easier to face your enemy when you have a clear picture of who he is, and what the strength of his forces are. I am honored that such an eminent doctor is willing to make the long trip here from Switzerland, with all of the important things that he must attend to. It says a great deal about the high regard he holds you in my son, and I am very proud that you have made such an impression on one of the leaders in your field."

Beppe looked at Paul, with the eyes of a proud father, grateful that he had such a fine reputation. "Well, enough of this gloom and doom. We have a fine bottle of Grappa here, and we are alive and together. We will be grateful for all of the Lord's blessings, and not quibble about tomorrow. We are here now, let tomorrow take care of itself." Beppe smiled at his family, and uncorked the bottle. If only he could save such moments in a bottle, with a very tight cork in it.

Over the course of the next few days there was much discussion and soul searching. The chapel saw increased activity, as every person on the Estate found some time to go into the small sanctuary. God heard from every member of the family, and their growing extended family.

The people of the hospital talked about the energetic man who was always at the heart of the town. They tried to think what they would do, if they were faced with a similar situation. The small chapel in the hospital saw a great deal of the staff over the next days, as they sought to ask for blessings from God for the Donat family, and looked for answers in their own lives. It seemed that bad things happened to good people, and it was hard to find reasons in their mind and hearts. Perhaps there was no reason, things just happen, and how we choose to deal with them is what will make them blessings or stumbling blocks.

The people of the town couldn't believe what they heard. Count Donat was indestructible! He had survived a war, and returned home to assume the title and responsibility for the region after his father died. He had worked tirelessly to help the area under his charge recover and prosper. He had seen them through the dark and frightening days of the last war. The Count had walked a precarious line with the Germans, to build up the hospital, and keep the worst of the fighting at bay. He was always looking for ways to improve the lives of the people of this area, and Lake Braies would be a much poorer place without him. They all remembered him and his family as they bowed their heads over their evening meals. They asked God to protect him.

There were many sleepless nights at the Castle while Beppe considered his options. He and Lucia talked and tried to understand what the right thing to do was. She would cry, and he would just hold her in his arms to give her what comfort he could. Guido and Beppe did the things that they usually did together, but now it seemed more intense and vital to them. Routine was comforting, and gave them an assurance that everything was as it should be, even though they knew it was not.

One afternoon, as Beppe and Guido sat outside in the garden playing their favorite game of cards, and drinking grappa, Guido finally had to give voice to the feelings of his heart. "Who could have thought all of those years ago, when we bumped into each other and spent the night talking on the train, that we would end up so well? I could never imagine that I would ever have a daughter, and a wife who loves me. That we would become so close, and always be there for each other. That our children would grow up and be married to each other, and that we would live to be grandpapa's?"

"You are right, my friend. There were so many dark days during the fighting that I never thought I would ever see Lucia again, or get to hold Paul in my arms. Now look at him, he has become a man, and has become a well respected doctor. He and Rita have given us such a gift in Francesco. I watch him and he seems to change every day, in front of my eyes. The world is a new place for me, as I see him discover things I had long taken for granted. I understand now how my own grandfather felt, and the joy just seems to fill me up. I hope that he will have some brothers and sisters, so he can be a big brother and teach them all of the wonderful things he has learned." Beppe had a wistful smile on his face, as he looked at Francesco sitting on the steps, watching a caterpillar crawling along next to his foot.

Guido watched Beppe's face, and knew what he was thinking—he was wondering if he would live to see any more grandchildren. "Do not worry, my friend, as they say, the bad herb never dies!" Guido tried to lighten the mood, and poured some wine into their glasses.

"You are right, of course, Sergeant Marron! I would have died long ago on that mountainside if it was not for you. I own every moment of every day since then to you, and what you sacrificed for me. The enemy dealt us a terrible blow that day, but we fought back and won the final victory. Now it would seem that they have come sneaking back all of these years later, looking to defeat us again. We faced them bravely then, and even though we have passed a lot of years and enjoyed a lot of Grappa, I don't think we will run like cowards now. I have two choices facing me, the way I see it. I can do nothing, and can wait to die. I can have the operation, and try to get this last gift from the Austrians out of my head, and have a chance to live. If I die, I have lost nothing; I am going to die anyway. I prefer to take a chance to live, and meet my enemy standing on my feet." Beppe looked at Guido, trying to gauge his reaction to the words that he had spoken. Somehow it made it seem more real, having finally said what he only felt in his heart.

"You don't owe me anything, *Captain* Donat," Guido laughed, using Beppe's rank to emphasize his point. "It could have as easily been you who knocked me out of the way that day. You would now have the crutches, and I would have the souvenir from the Austrians. Everything that I have received from that moment, I have because of you. You stayed on with me in Trento, when you could have come home to Lucia and Paul months earlier. You brought me into your home, and I became a part of your family. You helped me find my little Rita, and were there as I grieved for Maria. You and Lucia helped Anna and I get together. I can't imagine my life without either of them. Our children grew up together, and we have a beautiful grandson together. In my way of thinking, we are two lucky Alpinos. I will support any decision you make."

"Thank you Guido, I know I can count on you to be here if God does not have the same plans we do. It will be hardest on Paul, if I die. It is a terrible burden I am putting on him. He is a good doctor, and his teacher will come from Geneva to help him. He is willing to take the risk, to give me a chance to live. He is so young; he hasn't experienced the things we have in battle, and doesn't understand how things can go bad so fast. If I die, you have to be the one to help him understand and not be too hard on himself. He will be busy at the hospital, so you will need to see to it that the Estate keeps running. It will be Francesco's someday, and we need to ensure it will be something that he can be proud of. Now, let's see who is going to win this card game. The loser has to go get us another bottle of wine!" Beppe smiled, at ease with his decision. He knew that things would be all right if he didn't make it. They were a strong family, and strong families can face anything.

Beppe informed everyone at dinner that night, and they were somber as they listened to him. Lucia had tears, but she was proud that Beppe had chosen to fight to stay with her. Paul nodded, realizing it was up to him now, and the burden suddenly felt very heavy. He would make the call, first thing in the morning, to Dr. Muller in Geneva. There was no point delaying; the sooner they made the attempt, the better their chances of success. Rita looked at Beppe, holding Francesco on his lap, and couldn't imagine him not being here. His bright smile and infectious laugh was one of her earliest memories, when she met them at the convent. She couldn't have loved him more if he had been her own father. She worried about Guido, if Beppe died. The two of them were inseparable; it would be like losing half of Guido's own soul.

Three days later, the train pulled into the station at Lake Braies, carrying a very important passenger from Geneva. Paul was at the depot to meet him, and the two men exchanged a firm handshake, and polite conversation. They didn't have to talk about the serious nature of this visit; it had been very much on both of their minds. It was late in the day, so Paul just drove Max Muller to the Castle. The family wouldn't hear of him staying in town, and he was their honored guest. They had an enjoyable dinner together, and the good doctor had the privilege of meeting Paul's entire family. He seldom knew the families of his patients, and it gave this surgery new meaning, and a perspective that he seldom had.

Paul and Dr. Muller left for the hospital early the next morning, to do a final review of Beppe's records. The latest x-ray, taken a few days before didn't show any changes, although Beppe's headaches were becoming more frequent and lasting longer. The medication Paul had been giving him for the pain was becoming less effective, and he had to go to stronger medication. They worked through the day, insuring they had done everything to prepare for the surgery. They didn't want any surprises in the operating theater that would reduce their chances of a successful surgery.

The morning dawned with a glorious display of incredible colors, painted by a divine hand on the clouds. The day that everyone had dreaded was here, there was nothing else to be done, and nothing else to say. The family rode to the hospital together, requiring two cars because there were too many of them. Beppe was greeted by waves and good wishes from everyone he passed as the cars made their way down the driveway and onto the road. It would seem that everyone knew this was the big day, and made it a point to have business on the street of the town as they drove by. Beppe was very touched by the show of affection from so many people. He was at peace, like the lull before a battle. He had made all of his preparations, and was now waiting for what might be the last battle of his life.

The entire staff of the hospital met Beppe at the door, and all of them reached out to touch him and wish him well. He thanked them for their love and concern, and headed off to prepare for surgery. The family took up their posts in the lounge, trying to get comfortable for what they knew was going to be a very long surgery. Lucia sat with him until they rolled him away down the hall, so they could have every last possible minute together. There were tears and kisses and hugs and last waves, as the gurney disappeared through the doors. Then there was silence, and Donna Lucia, Anna, Guido and Rita assumed their various stations to wait. Francesco had remained at home with Nina, and had given his Grandfather a hug and a kiss and a big smile before they left.

The hours rolled by, and the hands of the clock barely seemed to move. They talked, and tried to keep each other company. They would get up and go to the small chapel in the hospital, to remind God of their request for Beppe's well being. They knew that Paul was having the most difficult time of them all, but at least he was there, and knew how things were going. They could only wonder and wait.

Finally Paul appeared at the door to the lounge, and he looked tired and spent. They all looked up expectantly, waiting for him to speak. "Father has survived the surgery, but it was worse that we could see on the x-rays. It was very deep, and it took a long time to reach it and ensure that we got the entire fragment out. He is in recovery now, and the next hours will be critical for him. We have done all that we can, it is up to God now. We will just have to wait and see."

Dr. Muller stayed on for the next three days, helping Paul monitor Beppe's vital signs and change his dressings. Beppe was in a coma, and the family took their turns sitting at his bedside. Guido would read to Beppe and whistle the old familiar tunes that he used to when Guido was in a coma in the hospital in Trento. He thought of those days, and was amazed how Beppe looked the same, with all of the bandages on his head. This time his beloved friend and brother did not find his way back to them by following his cheerful tunes. Count Giuseppe Donat quietly slipped out of the loving arms of his family and friends, a hero of Italy to the end.

Chapter Twenty-six

A dark cloud attended the entire region in the days to follow. The funeral Mass was held at the bigger Church in Lake Braies, because so many people wanted to pay their respects and say their final good-byes. There was a military honor guard in attendance at the funeral, and Beppe was buried in the family cemetery, alongside generations of his family before him. Donna Lucia was most thankful for all the outpouring of love and respect for her husband. She felt a grief beyond understanding, and it was only the love of her family and the company of her grandson that encouraged her to face a life without her beloved Beppe.

The family closed ranks, and supported each other. It was a balm for their own grief, to try and keep each other's spirits up. Paul now assumed the title of Count Donat, and he felt very inadequate to try and fill his father's shoes. The responsibilities of his father for the Estate and the lands now fell to him. Guido tried to assist him, along with other members of the staff, to keep up with the demands of the farms and gardens. Donna Lucia, accompanied by Anna, took fresh flowers to

Beppe's grave every day. She knew that she needed to be brave, and do her share to see to the needs of their region, but her heart was with Beppe. Rita was now the Countess Donat, and she tried to expand her roll of caring for the obligations of her noble family. She worried about Paul and her father and Lucia and Anna. They were all taking Beppe's death very hard. Francesco was the bright sunshine in all of their lives, and he was tireless in keeping them entertained and happy.

Paul was struggling to keep up with his work at the hospital and take care of the duties that his father and twenty generations of his ancestors had been responsible for. His first love was always medicine, but his strong sense of duty and love for his father forced him to split his loyalties. Rita did what she could to share the historic obligations of the family, and the effort left them both exhausted and drifting farther apart. There was little time to spend with each other, and they seldom had time to go for a walk anymore, much less talk about anything but the most important things in their hectic schedules.

It was a mere six months after Beppe's death that Donna Lucia lost her fight with her grief and loneliness. Another dark cloud had come to rest over the Castle, as they laid her to rest beside her beloved husband. Paul's grief at losing his mother, and the guilt that he still felt over the loss of his father really began to affect him. He knew rationally that he had done his best; Dr. Muller assured him that no one could have done any better. It was still hard for him to accept. He had helped so many other people, but he was unable to help his own father. His training as a Psychiatrist was of less use to him that his degree in neurology had been. He knew all of the symptoms of grief and guilt and loss, but when they came crashing onto him personally, he was powerless to help himself. Rita tried to comfort him, and he was grateful, but he became more and more emotionally distant from her.

Guido did his best to help Paul. They talked, and he shared Beppe's concerns and fears with Paul, if Beppe died. It gave comfort to Paul to hear his father's words, but he was still desolate that he couldn't save him, and felt like a failure.

Guido started to feel some pains in his back, but he thought that he was just doing too much. He would take some medicine, and an extra glass of grappa, but he couldn't hide his pain from Anna. She was concerned about him, he was not a young man any more, and the loss of his beloved friend weighed heavy on his heart. He seldom went to town any more, sending younger men to take their goods to market instead.

Anna finally talked to Rita about her concerns, and Rita began to keep a closer eye on her father. One afternoon, while she was in the garden with Francesco, Guido had a severe pain in his back that he could no longer pretend was not there. Anna stayed with Francesco, while Rita drove Guido to the hospital. Paul met them at the emergency entrance, and hurried his uncle into an examining room. He was very tender in the lower area of his back, and Paul gave him a shot for the pain before they sent him down to x-ray. The x-ray revealed a large mass on his liver, and a biopsy confirmed that it was cancer. It was long past the stage where it could have been treated, so they did what they could to keep Guido comfortable in the time that he had left.

Guido joined Beppe and Donna Lucia and his beloved Maria before the year was out. The black clouds had taken up residence in Lake Braies, and refused to go away. He was buried in the family cemetery, next to Beppe, another Hero Alpino of Italy finishing his last engagement. There were Alpinos from all over the region that came to say good-bye to a vanishing generation of their ranks. The younger Alpini could not understand the deep bond between these aging comrades. The old men had gone to war together, and had looked out for one another. The younger men, under the Fascist's regime, had been dispersed all over the army, and never knew the brotherhood that these men had enjoyed. Rita and Anna and Paul were very touched by the number of military of all ranks who came to pay tribute to a man who was among the very few to have earned Italy's high award for bravery. They sang the songs of the Alpini, songs that Guido had whistled so often. They spoke of a love for their mountains and their country and their homes. Rita could see her father and her uncle in her mind's eye, as they enjoyed the songs and the singing. They would both have been proud and honored, and felt unworthy of so much fuss.

Chapter Twenty-seven

After the death of her father, Rita began to feel more and more isolated. Anna stayed close to her, and the two women shared their grief together. Rita started to feel the walls of the Castle that she grew up in start to become more of a prison. Paul worked more and more hours, trying to keep up with his impossible schedule, and she felt like she needed something more than caring for Francesco to occupy her mind. She decided to return to work two days a week, to try and help improve her flagging spirits. Paul thought it was a good idea for her to get away from the Castle, and to give help to people who desperately needed her. He felt better when he was doing something for others; especially the patients who could least afford his care. He gave a great deal of time to working in the Free Clinic that he had named after his father, and it was a source of solace to see the good that it was doing. He was sure his father, mother, and his uncle Guido would approve of his efforts.

Things started to stabilize a little, and the people who called the Estate home started to breathe a little easier. It was still very difficult losing so many people that they loved, in such a short period of time. The clouds brooding on the horizon of the eternal mountains were not done testing the metal of this valiant family. The next spring saw a round of influenza that swept through the valley. It was very virulent, and there weren't many families that were not touched by its deadly fingers. The hospital was pressed to the breaking point, with so many people sick. Hospitals from all over Italy sent in extra doctors and nurses to try and fortify the staff at Lake Braies. This region was hit the hardest, and the death toll rose alarmingly. Anna came down sick, but recovered after a long period of time. Rita was starting to show symptoms when Francesco began to cough. Being so young, the small boy did not have the reserves to fight the deadly flu, and died a week after showing the first symptom.

One week Francesco was a happy child, playing and getting into mischief. The next week he was being buried in the cemetery with others who were sure to be waiting to welcome this dear child into their outstretched arms. He was the glue that held the last of Paul and Rita's fragile marriage together.

With the death of their son, they each headed off into their own personal hell. No parents should have to outlive their child. That was not the way of things. Parents could die, and there would be grief and sorrow, but the future was still waiting for their children. Paul and Rita were suddenly without a future, and they became virtual strangers. They were each probably blaming themselves for bringing down the judgments of God on their family. The secrets carried in each of their hearts made it impossible for them to comfort each other.

Chapter Twenty-eight

Rita was still weak from her bout with the flu, but could no longer bear the suffocating emptiness of the Castle. She and Paul barely spoke a word to each other at meals, when they ate at all. Anna did what she could, but the Castle had become a place of silence, anger, and despair.

Rita returned to nursing full time, trying to find enough work to numb her weary mind and her empty heart. She and Paul worked together, and did the things that they were expected to do, but they avoided talking to each other as much as they could. The hospital was still in the middle of the flu epidemic, and the new cases mounted up daily. It was inevitable that sooner or later Rita and Renato Pini would cross paths again. Rita had seen him a number of times, over the years since Paul had returned from Switzerland, but she had always been careful to avoid any appearance of impropriety. She was safe in her iron loyalty to her family, and the resolve she felt to keep her promises to Paul and to God.

Paul was now a stranger, a ghost who inhabited the same halls of the Castle that she did. She had tried to rely on the faith that had sustained her from her earliest memories, but the sudden death of Francesco was the grain of sand that pushed her over the edge. God, if He existed at all, had become a cruel Lord, and she couldn't find it in her heart to care what He thought, or what He expected from her any longer. All she had left was her work, and even though she was still weak from her own illness, she threw herself into it with a fierce will that frightened even her.

She was working in another ward, having just lost another patient, when she ran into Renato. It surprised her that she felt such pleasure in seeing him again. She didn't take joy in anything these days, and the sudden leap of her heart startled her. He looked just as tired and defeated as she did, and she was grateful for a break in the lounge for a cup of tea with an old friend. He said how sorry he was that she had had so much loss in her life this past year, especially the death of her son. She was grateful for his concern, but she had cried so much lately she had no tears left. They continued to talk, and it felt good to Rita to have a conversation with someone.

Paul had just finished with a long surgery, and was exhausted as he headed for his office. He was surprised that Rita wasn't there waiting for him. She was usually very prompt, ready to go home after a long day. He was the one who was usually late, so he asked the staff nurses if they had seen her. The replied that she was working on another ward this afternoon, and they hadn't seen her come back. He decided to go looking for her, and was surprised when he finally located her in the staff lounge, having a cup of tea with Dr. Pini. He almost spoke up right away, but held back a moment. Rita was having a good talk with the handsome doctor, and it was the most animated he had seen her in months. He tried not to read too much into it, but he couldn't help but envy the easy manner with which she spoke to him. Rita used to confide in him that way, but that was a long time ago, before all of the death and sadness that descended on the Castle.

"Rita," said Paul in a tired voice, "are you ready to go home? I was expecting to see you in my office, but they said that you were working in this ward today." Rita gave little start when she heard Paul's voice; she hadn't realized it was so late.

"I'm sorry, Paul," Rita managed, rising from her seat and spilling her tea. "I was so tired, a cup tea sounded good. We lost another patient this afternoon; that is the eighth this week. You remember Dr. Pini, don't you? He was on Dr. Kruger's staff here at the hospital about the same time I started working here."

"Yes, of course, nice to see you again, Dr. Pini." Paul held out his hand, as the other doctor rose to his feet for a proper greeting.

"It is good to see you as well Dr. Donat." Renato replied, careful to keep a neutral face. "I can't tell you how sad we all were when Francesco contracted this terrible flu and died. We are continuing to see the number of cases mount on a daily basis, and we don't seem to be able to do much to stop it."

"Thank you for your kind words," Paul replied, feeling tightness in his chest at the mention of his son's name. "I am afraid that there will be a great many more families that will cry before this epidemic eases up. It has the potential to be the worst one in a hundred years. It has been a long day for us, and we should be getting home."

"Of course, it was good to talk to you again, Rita, thank you for all of your help in this terrible crisis, in spite of your own loss." Dr. Pini smiled, nodded to them both, then headed out of the lounge to continue his duties.

Rita was careful not to follow Renato out the door with her eyes, and it made her nervous that Paul seemed a little more interested in him than he should have been. Paul was angry with himself for being so sensitive. He had to admit that he felt a little jealous that someone could talk to his wife and help to raise her spirits, when he failed so miserably. He was so intent on his own grief that he had buried himself in his work and his estate duties, largely ignoring Rita's needs. She had tried to talk with him several times since Francesco's funeral, but he had just shut her out. He felt ashamed of himself, but it was hard for him to find the words that he should have been able to say to her. He still loved Rita, but he was paralyzed when they were together. Perhaps he was feeling the guilt of his betrayal in his heart. He had always loved her more than she had loved him, he was sure of that. Rita had tried to be a good wife to him, but he was sorry that what they had was only friendship, the passion just wasn't there.

Over the coming days, he tried to be more attentive, but Rita didn't seem to respond to his efforts. Paul didn't blame her. If he had been so rejected; he doubted if he would be open and forgiving. He noticed that Rita seemed more content when they returned home, after working on the same ward that Dr. Pini worked on. Of course she had no control over where she was assigned, but a clear pattern was beginning to emerge in his tired mind.

Paul was sitting in his office one afternoon, finishing some reports when he looked out his window. He recognized Rita standing in the garden by the statue of the Madonna, and she seemed very upset about something. Her head was bowed, and her shoulders were hunched over. It looked like she was praying, or perhaps crying.

He was just getting to his feet to go outside and see what had happened when he saw Dr. Pini walk up behind her and say something. Rita whirled around and threw herself into his arms, crying uncontrollably. It stopped Paul short; something was very wrong, and Rita was clearly in distress, but all he could think about was this man holding his wife in his arms. It felt like it would burn a hole straight into his brain.

Paul headed outside on the run, unable to stop himself. He was afraid of what he would see in her eyes, but he couldn't force himself to forget what he had just witnessed. Rita looked up when she saw him running towards her, and immediately pushed herself away from the man who had been comforting her just a moment before. Her eyes were red from crying, but there was something else there, for an instant, and Paul would see it again over and over in his mind. "What's wrong, Rita, what's happened?" Paul finally reached them, waiting for an explanation, and held her hand. She was wiping her eyes, and still gulping in air trying to stop her sobbing, and get a hold of herself.

"Rita was taking care of a young boy in the ward—he has been there for several days now." Dr. Pini spoke up, seeing that Rita wasn't able to say anything. "She was holding him when he died, and it was just too much for her. His parents died last week, and there was no one to be there with him at the last."

Paul looked at Dr. Pini, and he could see the feelings this man had for Rita without being told. He felt an instant rage, but fought down any reaction. "Thank you for your concern, Dr. Pini, I can take care of her now. Paul put his arm around Rita, and guided her to his office. He got her a glass of water, and went to tell the nurses' station that he was taking Rita home. They had already heard what had happened, and they asked him to give Rita their best.

Rita was quiet on the drive home, and didn't seem to really know that Paul was there. He kept going over in his mind what he had seen in the garden, how easily she had gone to that man. She had never been that way with him, not even when he first arrived home from Switzerland.

Anna was outside when they got home, and was surprised to see them so early. Paul told Anna what happened, and she helped Rita into the house so she could lie down before dinner.

Paul went outside to sit in the garden, and try to calm his troubled mind. He just kept seeing Rita in Renato Pini's arms, like she was comfortable there, and he felt the envy and jealousy start to rise like bile in his throat. He had a doctorate in psychiatry, and he knew all of the clinical reasons for what he was feeling, but he couldn't stop the emotions that were crashing around inside his head. He watched a flock of pigeons picking their way through the far end of the garden, eating up some seeds here and there. Something startled them, and they all took off into flight, like they were flying in formation. He watched them with unexpected longing, and envied the freedom they had. They could fly off any time they chose, and they could go anywhere they pleased. Paul looked back at the spot they had just left, and noticed a large black bird sitting there. He was probably the reason the other birds had left in such a hurry. Black birds were not well liked by the avian community, robbing from other nests and stealing their food. They were intruders, and the harbingers of bad luck. It flew off and landed on the roof of the Castle, near their bedroom. He thought of Rita taking a nap inside, and he wondered if she were thinking about the man who had held her so familiarly in the garden a short while ago.

He would keep a closer eye on this situation. He didn't want to believe what he thought he had seen, after all Rita had been under a tremendous strain that would have broken a weaker person.

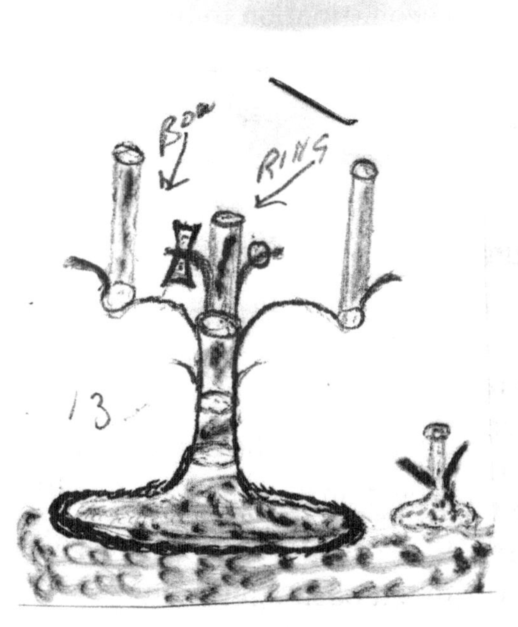
BOX
RING
13

Chapter Twenty-nine

He got the confirmation to his darkest fears about a week later. He had seen Rita heading for a supply room, and followed her. She looked over her shoulder before opening the door, and quickly went inside. The door had a small window in it, to keep someone inside from opening the door unexpectedly and colliding with someone outside by accident. He could just make out the back of Rita's head, and there was someone else in there with her. He waited for a few minutes, until Rita came out again, heading back to the nurses' station. He ducked out of sight so she didn't see him, and continued to keep an eye on the door. His patience finally paid off, and Dr. Renato Pini emerged from the door, also looking around before he headed off in the other direction. Paul closed his eyes for a moment, as the weight of what he had seen settled in on him. Then he turned and took a shortcut to his office, knowing Rita would be showing up soon for their ride home.

"How was your afternoon?" Asked Paul, noticing how calm and in control Rita seemed. "Was there anything interesting on the ward today?"

"Nothing out of the ordinary," Rita replied quietly, looking out of the window at the statue of the Madonna in the Garden. "What about you, how is that new patient that they brought in this morning doing?"

"He had a nasty bump on his head, but I think he will be fine. He is resting comfortably, and we will keep him for the night. If he is doing all right in the morning, we will probably let him go home. We are so short on beds right now, we can't keep patients as long as we would like.

I had a call from Dr. Muller this afternoon. He has a good friend in Verona he is worried about, and he can't get away to attend to him. He was hoping that I would be able to go and see him, and I said that I would. I could hardly refuse him; after all of the trouble he went to when father was ill." Paul made a show of putting some additional supplies into his black bag, as if he were really preparing to go and visit a patient. "It is pretty late in the day, so I'll leave in the morning. I don't know what I will run into, but I should be home by Monday at the latest." With that, Paul picked up his bag, and he and Rita went home.

The next morning, Paul finished his breakfast. He seemed unusually preoccupied, and Anna was wondering why he seemed so distracted. He didn't respond to Anna's goodbye, which she thought was very odd. Rita seemed unusually happy this morning, and didn't seem to notice that Paul didn't say good bye to them as he left for his trip.

Rita was thinking about how she might take advantage of this rare opportunity, as Paul was seldom out of town on business. She prepared to go to work at the hospital, like always. They were so understaffed due to the flu epidemic, that it was normal for her to work on the weekends, every available nurse did. She would see Renato at break and let him know that Paul was out of town. They could discuss finding a way to be together, without being seen. The both of them were well known, and it would cause a big scandal if they were seen together, with Paul out of town.

About midnight, long after everyone at the Castle was asleep, Rita slipped out a rear door, keeping to the shadows. There was a full moon, and she didn't want to be seen making her way across the lawn. She kept well out of sight, until she came to the long boulevard at the end of the driveway. There was a car parked in the shadows. Renato Pini was waiting for her, scarcely believing that she would be with him tonight. He had long ago given up the hope of being something more than her friend, since Dr. Kruger had spoken to him before he departed for Germany. The doctor had warned him it was for the best if he didn't pursue his attraction for Rita. The Donats were a much loved and admired family, and he didn't want to do anything that would cause Rita grief.

When she finally reached the car, they drove off quietly, not wanting to make a lot of noise. They took a longer way into town, keeping to the less traveled lanes. They didn't see anyone at this hour, but they didn't let their guard down. Renato let Rita out in a wooded area near her father's old apartment, and drove off to conceal his car. He knew that dark streets still have eyes, remembering what Rita had said about her Grandma Delia seeing them the last time they were at Guido's small apartment. He came from another direction, being careful to keep to the shadows. He knocked quietly at the door, and Rita let him in. She looked at the small apartment across the alleyway. Her Grandma Delia had passed away several years earlier, but Anna still owned the house. It had too many memories for her to want to part with it. She still went there on occasion, when she was sad and missing Guido, or her mother.

After about ten minutes, another shadow appeared in the alley, and made its way to the door. The door opened and closed quietly, as the shadow went inside. Paul Donat paused, and listened for a moment, and then headed up the stairs. Rita and Renato were standing in the moonlight, locked in a passionate embrace. They both turned at the sound of a creak on the stairs, and were shocked to see Paul standing there. They froze, not knowing what to do.

Paul was the first one to speak, after a very long silence. "What, don't you have anything to say?" Paul just stood there in his rage. Rita just lowered her head and looked away from him.

"We have no excuse for our behavior. We fell in love with each other during the war, while you were in

Switzerland. Rita didn't know if you were coming back, or how you would feel about her when you did."

"That may have been so before I returned, but now she is my wife. That must surely mean something to you, if obviously not to her." Paul challenged the man standing next to his wife. "This is appalling behavior for a man dedicated to easing the suffering of others, Dr. Pini. You will get dressed immediately and get your things together and leave this city tonight, forever. I will make your apologies at the hospital in the morning. You had an unexpected emergency at home in Trento, and had to leave with haste. You will write an appropriate letter in a few days letting the administration of the hospital know you will not be able to return. I am a Count, and my family has ruled this region for over four hundred years. I will not allow a scandal to stain the good reputation of my family, so this matter ends here. Now go."

"No!" cried out Rita, finally able to speak. "I am sorry I have hurt you Paul, but you must admit that we were never truly in love. We have loved each other, but we have never been in love. I won't make any trouble, just let me go with Renato tonight, and you will never see or hear from me again. You can tell people whatever you want, that is up to you. I love the family as much as you do, and I don't want to hurt them either. I have loved you as my brother, and I was wrong to let the expectation of our parents persuade me to marry you."

"I can imagine what our parents and our son are thinking about that sad excuse right now, looking down at you from heaven. No, you will stay; there would be too many questions, and no answer that would make any sense. I have always admired your elegance and taste, Dr. Pini," said Paul, reaching down to pick something up off of the table next to him. "I will just keep these as souvenirs for my wife, to remember you after you have gone." Paul held up a class ring from Renato's University in Milan, and the tie he had been wearing.

Renato knew there was no other choice. Paul was well within his rights as a husband who had just caught him with his wife, or the ruler of this region. Royalty did not have the same power it once enjoyed several hundred years ago, but an order from a Count to leave his holdings was still lawful and binding. Renato nodded, gave one sad look over Paul's shoulder to Rita, and headed down the stairs and out the door.

Paul and Rita left a few minutes later, like two strangers who had never met. The silence between them was like a tangible black cloud, a cloud that had been gathering over the Castle to take permanent possession. When they arrived in the moonlit shadows, Rita went to her room and locked the door. She would need the time to prepare to face the staff, to pretend that nothing had happened.

Anna was surprised to see Paul in the morning. He had left for Verona, and suddenly he was back. Anna could feel the tension in the air, and she knew that something had happened. Rita came down, ready to attend Mass, but she and Paul kept a distance between them. Rita wore a veil over her head that extended down to her cheeks. Anna couldn't see her expression, but she knew that she had been crying. She and Paul attended church, as they did every Sunday morning, unless they had to work at the hospital. They sat where they always did, but Anna wasn't fooled. There was a wall between them, just a real as if it had been built out of the same stones of this old church.

Rita was praying for forgiveness for her weakness. She was sorry she had not been strong enough to disappoint her family and not marry Paul. It was a lie, and the lie only got larger and heavier with each passing year. This year, with the loss of so many people she held dear had finally broken her, especially when God took Francesco away from her. He had been her sole consolation for all of the empty years she had endured. When he died, she lost her last reason to honor this ill conceived vow that she had made to God, and to Paul, in front of her family and friends in this holy place. The world was a place that she no longer belonged to, and she had made up her mind that she would leave and go back to the convent.

Paul was unworthy to reside in the Castle that had held so much meaning in the lives of his Donat ancestors. All he could think of was Rita's betrayal and his desire for revenge. He was glad he had made Renato Pini leave like a whipped dog. It had given him great satisfaction to finally be able to use the power of his title at last.

After Mass, Paul greeted everyone there, just like he always did. Rita tried to follow suit, and most people probably thought she was just tired from all of the hours she was putting in at the hospital. She had been ill with the flu as well, and it had drained her reserves. Surely she would have stayed home to recuperate longer, if she were not grieving over the death of their son. Everyone understood her desire to stay busy, and be of service to those who still had great need of her skill and training. She was the Countess now, and she took her duties very seriously, even at the expense of her own health. She was greatly loved and admired by all who knew her.

When everyone had gone, Paul invited Anna and Rita to take a walk with him. Rita didn't show any emotion, and Anna had a very bad feeling about this. The flowers were beautiful and their fragrance filled the air, but Anna couldn't smell them. She could feel the black cloud that had followed them from the church, and that was all she could concentrate on. Rita just walked along next to her, without saying a word.

"Anna" began Paul, after she and Rita took a seat under the Gazebo by the lake, "I have always loved you, and you have been a big part of my life. You and Uncle Guido were so special to me, and I miss him very much. This is a very important place to me, it is where Rita and I spent our last few hours together, before I left for Switzerland. We spoke about the possibility of getting married here. Things have been strained this last year, with the deaths of four people we all loved very much. I have had an uneasy feeling of late, and my fears were confirmed last night when I caught Rita and Dr. Renato Pini together at Uncle Guido's old apartment in town. Anna looked at Rita with shock and dismay, but Rita sat still next to her as if she had turned to stone. She looked at Paul, and she didn't like the smug look of triumph on his face. What kind of monster could take pleasure in the suffering of someone he was supposed to love?

Rita answered Paul coldly, as if it was someone else who spoke. "Yes Paul, we made promises to each other here, and I am your wife. We had a marriage to make our parents happy, but it was a marriage without the love that we should have had. I was content, because I felt guilty wanting more, when all around us was death and misery. God blessed us with a son, and finally I felt He was repaying me for what I should have had, instead of what I allowed myself to settle for. The ties that bound us together were broken when Francesco died. Your parents and my father were gone. The best reason I had for continuing to deny myself any real happiness was lowered into a grave near theirs. End this unhappy charade and let me go, there isn't any point in my staying any more!"

"No!" replied Paul coldly. "You are my wife, and we will uphold the vows we made to God. We did not promise to stay together until we didn't love each other anymore. We agreed, of our own free will and choice, to stay together until death parts us, and that is what we are going to do. I do not want to bring shame and scandal to the noble name of our family, so you will stay, and we will all remain here. You may have your own room, and you never have to come to my bed again. I only ask that we sit together at dinner time, which will be expected by the staff."

"All right," said Rita, with no life in her voice. "I will sit with you at dinner, and I will take care of the duties of our calling." Rita was thinking that is probably justice from God, and she would accept her punishment.

As Paul turned to go he turned back to Anna, and dug something out of his vest pocket. "I wanted to return these keys to your mother's apartment; I borrowed it for a few hours last night." Anna looked after Paul in shock, staring at the keys in her hand. She wondered what had happened to the beautiful little boy she had come there to help care for, there was no evidence that he still existed. Anger and jealousy had turned him into someone she didn't recognize, and she was glad that Beppe and Guido had not lived to see the kind of man he had become. They were so kind and caring; it would have been a great sadness for them to see him now. She prayed to God that this whole unfortunate situation would not destroy both of their souls. She blamed herself for allowing Rita to go through with this marriage, just to make her family happy. If God were looking for someone to blame, then she was praying He would take it out on her instead of them.

Rita and Anna were seated at the dining room table when Paul arrived. He had a very self satisfied look on his face when he saw that they were here as promised. He reached into his pocket and pulled out a black bow tie, with a good ring attached to it. "I thought the dining room table could use a little dressing up; it seems to me it is looking a little plain lately. He reached over, hanging the tie on the silver candlestick next to Rita. Renato's ring hit the candle stick, as Paul pulled his hand away, making a metallic sound. He apparently liked the sound, because he reached back over, and shook the candle stick, making the noise again. Anna could see Rita stiffen up, but she didn't look at Paul, or say a word. Paul wasn't going to let the opportunity to take a dig a Rita pass and added, "I think it will be a nice reminder of people we wish were here, but are needed elsewhere."

Anna just stared at Paul, not believing the transition she was seeing before her eyes. Rita just took the whole matter stoically, and refused to say anything. Anna thought that Rita felt she deserved it, and was taking her punishment without complaint. As soon as dinner was over, Rita rose to her feet and walked out of the dining room and went straight to her room.

Chapter Thirty

The days took a familiar pattern; Rita would take care of the business of the Estate, until Paul got home from the hospital. She would then go to her room and wait until the appointed hour for the evening meal, and take her place at the table. Paul would chat away about his day at the hospital, and Rita would listen without comment. She endured his snide remarks, and the bow tie that continued to hang on the candle stick, without defending herself, or fighting back. As soon as dinner was over, she would rise and go to her room.

The days began to take their toll, as Rita grew increasingly thinner and thinner. Anna never saw her smile while Paul was away at the hospital. The things she used to enjoy went unnoticed as she bravely tried to take care of the business of the Estate that her Uncle Beppe and her father had loved so much. The two of them had worked together, side by side, through good times and bad, to take care of this sacred trust from Beppe's ancestors. She intended to do her best to follow their example, to honor their memory.

Anna tried to get Rita to eat a little something during the day, but Rita wasn't interested. She still tried to eat a little at dinner, to keep up appearances, but even that effort was waning. Paul was getting less and less satisfaction from the revenge he felt was his due. Rita just sat quietly at dinner, night after night, not showing the slightest bit of retaliation, no matter what the provocation. She just listened politely to whatever he had to say, and then went to her room after the meal was over.

Now that he had gotten over the sure conformation that his wife preferred another man to him, other thoughts were starting to surface in his mind. Paul began to think about the few words Rita had said before she fell silent, and they picked up weight each day. He had always known that he loved her more than she loved him. Thinking back to the night before he left, he realized that she had sacrificed herself to make him happy. She had no way of knowing if they would ever see each other again, and like her mother, she wanted to send Paul off to meet the unknown with a full heart. He could see that now, that she had cared more for his happiness than her own. When he returned from Switzerland, it had been the same. He knew now that she had stumbled upon true happiness, under the pressure of death and misery all around her. She had sacrificed herself again for him, pushing away a love she longed for, to make him happy and to make the rest of the family happy. He had blinded himself to what was really happening, because he didn't want to know the truth. He had what he wanted, and that was all that mattered to him.

Then there was the matter of Janet Muller. Paul knew what a hypocrite he had been; punishing Rita for a sin he was even more so guilty of. He could have stayed in Geneva and married Janet. Rita would have understood, but never his parents. He was expected to come home and assume the title and the Estate, when his father thought he was ready. He had hurt two good women, to feed his blind devotion to his family, and push for a love that could never be. He decided that he would ease up on Rita, and make a clean breast of the brooding conscience that followed him up and down the halls of the hospital.

When he came home that night, only Anna was at the dinner table. "Where is Rita this evening?" asked Paul, looking around to see if she might be on her way.

"She wasn't feeling very well this evening, so she went to bed early; she hoped you wouldn't mind," Anna replied, not offering any other explanation. Paul knew she had grown to hate him for what he had put Rita through, and to be honest he didn't blame her. It was becoming more difficult to look at himself in the mirror every morning when he shaved.

Rita continued to be a no-show at dinner, and Paul didn't force the issue, knowing how badly he had behaved. Perhaps if he stopped enforcing his dinner edict, Rita would forgive him, and come back to the table on her own. Rita was due this small sign of respect, after all that he had put her through.

Anna helplessly watched Rita grow weaker day after day. She would take some warm milk and biscuits up to her each morning, hoping to get her to eat a little something. Rita just smiled weakly and patted her hand. She wouldn't allow Anna to tell Paul what was really going on, and Anna was the only one at the Castle that was allowed to see Rita.

The autumn cold arrived early that year, taking with it the beautiful flowers that Anna would bring to Rita's room every day to try and cheer her up. The birds had gone with the cold fingers that gripped the Castle, taking with them their song and their colorful feathers as they would sit on the branches outside of Rita's window. The lake was a flat dead color, reflecting the black clouds that hung over the Estate. The wind howled a mournful sound, as it sailed past the eaves.

The morning that Anna had fought against finally arrived. She had taken Rita's breakfast tray up to her room like she always did, but this morning was different. Rita did not raise her head in greeting, her eyes were closed, and she lay deathly still. Anna dropped the tray from her numb fingers, and ran to her side, to see if she was still alive. Rita was still breathing, but her breaths were shallow and irregular. Anna was frightened that the last person she loved in this world was preparing to leave her, too. She had promised Rita that she wouldn't inform Paul of her true condition, but Rita was unconscious now, and she couldn't object.

Anna had a little revenge of her own in mind, and she descended the stairs in a rush. The anger that had been building up in her heart, since Paul had announced Rita's infidelity, had come to a full boil. She was prepared to deliver it now, with a knife sharper than any scalpel.

Anna picked up the phone, and dialed the hospital. She could hear the phone ringing, and Paul himself answered on the forth ring. She hardly recognized her own voice when she spoke into the receiver; it was cold and professional. "Noble Doctor, Count Paul Donat," said Anna, feeling very much like the stranger she had become. "This is Mrs. Guido Marron. If you would like to speak to your wife, I suggest that you come home immediately. She is dying, and I am sure there are a few more evil things you would like to say to her, before she goes to be with those who still love her." With that Anna put the receiver back on its cradle, and walked back up the stairs to wait with Rita, until she was free of this misery.

Paul sat and stared at the phone in his hand in shocked disbelief. He had though Rita was just sick of the sight of him, and he would respect her privacy. He knew Anna had spoken the truth, and there was no doubt in his mind that she hated him to the core of her soul at this very moment. She would have to wait in line to unleash the anger that was in her heart, because he hated himself so much more than she could ever begin to. He called a man he considered a miracle worker when people were in such a dire condition as Rita. He almost wept with relief when he heard the voice of his friend, Dr. Elio Tanzio, answer the phone.

"Elio," began Paul in a stricken voice he didn't have to fake, "This is Paul Donat. I have just received a call from home that my wife is gravely ill, and I need you to come at once. I'm going to get my car immediately; please join me as soon as you can gather your supplies. I will be waiting at the Emergency Entrance for you. Please hurry!"

"Yes, of course Paul, I'll be there without delay." Dr. Tanzio said, catching the urgency in Paul's voice. He started to ask for some details about Rita's condition, but the phone was already dead.

Paul bolted out the door of his office, almost knocking over two interns and a resident heading off on their rounds. He didn't even bother to offer an explanation, or his apologies for his unseemly haste, he just headed for the exit at a dead run. The staff all looked at him in amazement, never seeing the eminent surgeon act like this even under the direst emergency.

Their confusion was satisfied, a little, when Dr Tanzio made his way for the door, a few minutes behind Dr. Donat. He was carrying a full medical kit, not knowing what he would be running into. He could clearly see the staff's puzzled expression, guessing that his friend Paul had already exited the hospital ahead of him. "We have just received word from the Castle that Countess Donat is gravely ill. I can only speculate that she has suffered some kind of relapse from the flu that she had earlier. She returned to work much too soon after her illness, and I am guessing it has caught up with her." With that he followed Paul out the door, leaving their staff with very somber expressions. There had already been too many deaths credited to this terrible flu; they couldn't bear the thought that it might now be preparing to claim one of their own.

Paul was waiting at the Emergency entrance for his friend, with the engine running. He was clearly distressed, and hit the accelerator as soon as Dr. Tanzio had shut the door. The two of them had been friends a great many years, and Paul confessed everything to him that had been going on between him and Rita. Paul was driving at top speed as he unburdened his soul to Tanzio, grimly determined that the Angel of Death would not beat him to Rita's bedside. Elio listened in silence, unable to believe that his friend was capable of such cruelty, no matter what the provocation.

"I have been so wrong! God can't look at me, and the devil himself wouldn't want my soul. It just made me crazy to see Rita in another man's arms. You have to do everything you can to save her, Elio, she can't die! I have to make this right. Please God, don't let her die! I have loved her since the day she came to live with us, and I have never truly loved anyone but her. I was hurt that she couldn't love me in return, the way I loved her. Now I can see that she loved me more than I ever could have imagined. I have to get to her and make this right. She never deserved any of this, it was all my fault. If there is a just God in Heaven, she will live, so I can tell her I am sorry.

Paul and Elio finally turned off of the main road and onto the gravel driveway, leading up to the Castle. Nina heard the car approaching, and met them at the door. Paul grabbed an armful of the medical supplies out of the car and his friend got the rest. He and Elio had their hands full as they climbed up the long staircase to Rita's room. Paul didn't go in, not wanting to interfere with the doctor's evaluation and treatment of Rita. He paused at the door, then turned and went down the stairs again. He went into the great hall, and sat down in the large leather chair by the fireplace, to wait for his findings.

Dr. Tanzio paused before approaching Rita lying on the bed. She was so still and pale he had to watch closely to assure himself that she was still alive. It had been his experience that when someone called to report an emergency, many times the person putting in the call overstated the severity of the case. He could see now, in this instance, it was understated. He opened his cases and started unpacking his equipment, with an uneasy feeling in his stomach that he would not have enough time. He set up the stands, and prepared to start the IV's that he hoped would buy him some time. He adjusted the drip rate to speed some liquids and nutrients into Rita's system as quickly as possible. To be sure, she was showing dangerous signs of dehydration, and the drip would help alleviate that first. The other part was not going to be as easy. He could see that she had not been eating very much for quite some time, and there were clear indications of malnutrition and outright starvation. It looked to him that she had just given up hope, and was waiting patiently for death to find her. While he was busy, attending to Rita, Dr. Tanzio caught a slight movement out of the corner of his eye. He turned to see Anna Marron, Rita's stepmother, standing in the corner of the room, obviously trying to stay out of the way.

"Do you think you will be able to help her, Doctor?" Anna asked, with a faint glimmer of hope in her eyes. "I have tried everything I know to get her to eat, even a little bread and milk, but she just smiled at me and shook her head."

"It is evident this has been going on over a long period of time. I am trying to get some fluids back into her veins; you were right to call when you did. If she had gone on too much longer, her heart would have simply stopped beating. I have done everything that can be done for now, we will just have to wait and see if she is able to respond. In cases like these, the deciding factor is the patient themselves. If there is a strong desire to live, they will usually pull through. Looking at her now, I am not optimistic that Rita wants to live." Dr. Tanzio spoke as gently as he could to Anna, because he could see that Rita meant a great deal to her.

Anna headed out the door, intending to administer a second dose of venom to the man who was waiting down stairs. When she went into the great room, Paul was sitting silently, staring into the fire. Physically he looked a great deal better than Rita did, but the look in his eyes spoke of the same tortured soul. He didn't look up until she was almost next to him; she could have reached out and struck him, but she decided her words would leave a more lasting impression.

"I see you have taken my advice and returned home immediately. It would be a shame for you to have worked so long to murder your wife, and not be here for the end. Your plan to shame and humiliate her was truly inspired. All you had to do was plant the seeds of destruction in her heart, and she helped you carry out your brilliant design. I look at you and I can't see the little boy that I used to love. It disgusts me to see what you have become. Some evil demon must have taken the real Paul Donat when he was still an infant. In his place he left the devil's spawn, to be raised by these unsuspecting noble people. God was merciful to take Beppe and Lucia and Guido to spare them from seeing this day. I wished He had taken me too, but He knew that Rita would need at least one person left here, if she would have any chance at all of surviving." Anna stared at Paul, wishing he would fight back; she was spoiling to really get into it with him. He just sat there like a whipped dog, not even flinching when the blows of her words struck him repeatedly.

Paul was in a far darker place than Anna could ever dispatch him to, with her words or her angry stares. He was desperately trying to think of a way he could help, something he could do to make Rita want to fight to live. He knew if he couldn't come up with something, and soon, his friend upstairs was just delaying the inevitable. The body cannot fight against the heart; it will follow where the heart takes it, no matter what is done to stop it.

After what seemed like an eternity, Tanzio appeared in the room, and sat down in the chair opposite Paul. Anna saw his approach as he descended the stairs, and quickly made her way back to Rita's room. Her place was with Rita, and she didn't want her to be alone when the end came for her. She had come here all those years ago to care for this energetic loving child of an old friend, and she would not fail to do her duty until the last.

Paul stirred, seeing something that sparked his interest for the first time in the hours that his friend had been upstairs with Rita. "How is she?" Paul blurted out, not able to wait a moment longer for the news he feared was coming.

"I have seldom seen someone in as serious a condition as your wife, and still be alive. I have given her fluids and nutrients that can be easily absorbed by her body. She must have been sliding for quite some time, to be as emaciated as she is. I have seen people in the grip of a famine that are better off than Rita. If I recall, your family has a chapel here on the Estate. You should go there and ask for God's help with her; I have done all I can. Now it is up to God, and Rita. I think you have broken the most sacred trust we are given when we become doctors. We are charged, and give our solemn oath, that we will do all in our power to preserve life. We are told to "Do no harm," in our Hippocratic Oath. You have failed, Paul. What you did to her—it would have been more merciful if you had just plunged a knife into her heart. At least her death would have been quick and easy. Starvation is a slow and lingering death. I would have serious doubts about you being able to carry on as a physician, after what I have just witnessed upstairs."

"I appreciate what you have done for her, and your words are not nearly as harsh a censure as I deserve. I haven't seen her in weeks, I had no idea what was happening. Ignorance is no defense; I set out to hurt her, and I have only succeeded in hurting everyone in the process. It is no wonder the devil uses jealousy to overcome the heart; it makes you blind and deaf and stupid. You can't see what you are doing, until it is too late to stop. It must be a nice bonus for him, the same emotion that enrages the user will end up killing him with remorse in the end. He is truly a master at what he does." Paul got up, and took his friend's advice. God might not be willing to listen to him, but at least he would go and make the attempt.

The chapel was cold, but the windows let the sun come streaming into the old stone sanctuary. As he sat there on a bench that he had sat on hundreds of times before, he really took a good look around. The stones had been rough hewed by hand, almost six hundred years before. He could see the skill of the masons, as they carefully made each stone as close to the same size as the next stone. There were stained glass windows near the front by the altar that defused the rays of light into colorful patterns and hues.

He thought about the history of this place. It had been a place of joyous weddings, and tearful funerals. There were countless babies blessed here, and times like this where people had assembled to bargain and plead with God for a loved one's life. This room had stoically endured the march of time, and had been whatever people expected it to be. It was just a large room, with no meaning of its own. Paul could almost hear the stones asking, "What is it you need from me?"

What did God expect Paul to be? He had entrusted one of his most precious daughters into his care, and he had failed her badly. What could he do for her now? He felt like the speckled gray stone that surrounded him, and he could hear his own voice asking, "What is it she needs from me? What can I do for her now?" Paul sat there, with his head in his hands, listening to that question over and over again in his mind.

His Guardian Angel must not have turned his back on Paul yet. He jumped up, with a flash of inspiration, and raced back for the Castle, as if Rita's life depended on him. It did depend on him. He had been so selfish and self centered, even now; he was only considering his own grief if he failed.

He grabbed the phone as soon as his fingers were close enough to reach it. He called the main number for the hospital, having called it so often he knew it as well as his own name. "This is Dr. Donat, I need the number for the hospital in Trento, it's an emergency!" The person who answered must have been used to such requests, and gave him the number without delay. He dialed the number, and waited for the line to connect. "This is Dr. Paul Donat from the Lake Braies Hospital, this is an emergency. It is imperative that I reach Dr. Renato Pini in Internal Medicine at once!"

After a short time, Dr. Pini answered. "This is Dr. Pini, what is the nature of the emergency?" Renato was all business, used to dealing with critical situations. The crisis that was about to present itself caught him completely off guard.

"Renato, this is Paul Donat, I don't have time for formalities. It is urgent that you come at once. Rita is in grave condition, near death, and it may help her if she can hear your voice. She is on an IV and we are doing all that we can. I believe that you are the one who can help tip the scales in her favor; her life is hanging in the balance." Paul waited, hoping against hope that Pini would not refuse him, after the way he had treated him.

"Dear God in Heaven! Thank you for calling, I am leaving immediately! Tell Rita I am on my way." Renato spun around, his mind racing. He had to get the resident on duty to cover his patients, and tell the Administrator he had to go. It really didn't matter what he said, it was merely a courtesy. He could fire him on the spot, for all he cared. If it was bad enough for Paul Donat to call and ask for his help, yesterday wasn't soon enough for him to get to Lake Braies to be with Rita.

The dark clouds that had fallen on the Castle, and refused to leave, were starting to break up. There was terrible lightning and thunder that would have awakened the dead themselves. The wind lashed the stones of the walls with their fury, and the rain poured off the roof, as if it were trying to cleanse the ancient structure from some dreadful plague.

It would be hours yet for Renato Pini to make it here from Trento, but at least he was on his way. He told Anna what he had done, and then went into the dining room for something he needed. He retrieved the scrap of black material holding the gold ring, still hanging from the silver candlestick where he had placed it. He had used it to punish Rita before, now he hoped he could use it to save her. The ring was like the stone walls of the Chapel, it would be whatever he wanted it to be.

He raced back up the stairs, and went to Rita's side. He was shocked to see her surrounded by tubes and stainless steel stands. She looked so small and fragile, with little more color than the white sheet that she was laying on. He pushed past his own feelings, and went over to her bedside and knelt down on the floor by her. He reached over and took her hand, careful not to disturb the tube that was fighting to give her a chance to live. He placed the ring gently in her hand, and closed her fingers around it. Then he began to pour out his soul to her. He remembered that his Uncle Guido used to read and whistle to his father, during the long days of his coma. Guido was sure that Beppe could hear him, so he continued, even when those who were in a position to know better told him he was wasting his time. "Too bad," Uncle Guido had said. "It is my time to waste!"

In those hours when the rain and lightening pounded the Castle, fighting to get in, Paul remained on his knees. He continued holding Rita's hand, and gave her the heart that had always belonged to her. He recounted his earliest memory of her, and their childhood together. He spoke of his love for her, and the lonely years he had spent away from her. He talked of everything he could think of, everything that she should hear, and prayed that she would indeed hear him. He was still on his knees, bathing her hand with his tears, when Anna brought Renato to Rita's room. Paul could barely get to his feet since the circulation in his legs had long ago given up on trying to attract his attention.

"Thank you for coming so quickly; she is still in a coma, but I believe she can hear us. Go and talk to her, let her hear your voice. My father once found his way back out of the black fog of a profound coma. Papa was following the sound of my uncle Guido, as he whistled a mountain tune. I know she is still in there; she may make it back if she hears your voice, and perhaps smell your cologne. Familiar happy things are vital for someone teetering on the edge, like Rita is. I was wrong to try and keep Rita with me, when her heart was always with you. I pray it is not too late, and between the two of us, we can still make this right."

Paul retreated over to the corner, where Anna and Elio were standing. The three of them stood there like sentinels, barring the Angel of Death from entering the door with their own bodies. Renato knelt down next to Rita, where Paul had spent so many hours, and started to talk to her. He called her by name, and begged her to come back to him. He kissed her hands and her face, desperately trying to reach her.

For long agonizing minutes there was no response, just the sound of the ticking from the great clock in her room. Renato fought for her life, as Paul and Elio Tanzio had before him. There was a quiet groan that froze everyone in their tracks, not daring to breathe. Had they really heard her, or were they so desperate that their imaginations were toying with them? Rita groaned again, this time moving her head slightly on her pillow. Her lashes briefly fluttered, and then she slowly opened her eyes. It looked like she was having a hard time focusing, and finally looked in the direction of Renato. "Is that really you?" Rita asked weakly, blinking to try and clear her vision.

"Yes, Rita, I'm here. Everything is going to be fine, just rest, my love." He looked at her like he was afraid she would vanish right before his eyes. She smiled at him weakly, and then closed her eyes again. Dr. Tanzio stepped up next to Rita's bed, on the other side, and listened to her heartbeat with his stethoscope. He smiled and nodded to the worried people standing behind him. Surprised she was not dead.

"I think we have passed the crisis point. She is very weak, but I believe that she has a good chance of recovery now. This is the first moment I have had any hope since I walked into this room!" Elio smiled at Paul and Anna, tired but satisfied with a long night's work.

Chapter Thirty-one

The dawn was beginning to break, as the sun triumphed over the clouds. The storm had spent its fury, and the clouds dissipated, having allowed their moisture to bless the soil. The bells in the tower of the old chapel began to ring out, seeming to peal out the joyous news that the Countess, Rita Donat, would live. The sound of the bells roused Rita again, and she opened her eyes. She seemed steadier this time, and more aware of her surroundings. She looked over at Renato, taking a moment before she spoke. "Is it really you? I have had the strangest dreams." Rita smiled over at Renato, able to feel his hand in hers, and felt the ring there. She looked down at it, still attached to the bow tie, and wondered.

"I am really here, and I will be with you until you send me away." Renato smiled at her through his tears, kissing her hand.

"Where is Paul? I dreamed he was here with me, only it was the real Paul this time. The other Paul was a demon who tried to fool us, but we should have known that it wasn't him. I am ashamed that he almost fooled me too! Now I know that my best friend has returned, and chased the demon back to that endless lake of fire and brimstone, where he belongs." Rita looked around the room expectantly, eager for the sight of her brother, who had been away for so long.

"Why are the bells still ringing?" asked Dr. Tanzio, as he headed downstairs to look for Paul. He didn't see him in the great room, so he decided to go see about the bells. He made his way to the Chapel tower, and called up the stairs. The two gardeners who were up there, pulling wildly on the ropes, finally heard him holler and came down. "What is the meaning of this? Why are you ringing the bells?"

"Count Donat sent us up here to ring the bells. He said that Donna Rita was ill, and she needed to hear the bells to help her come back to us. He said to ring the bells until we died or she did!" The taller of the two gardeners looked at the doctor, hoping for more answers than they had gotten from the Count.

"He was right, she was very ill. She heard the bells and woke up. I think she will recover now. Thank you for the bells, now the whole valley will know that she is going to be all right. Have you seen the Count?" inquired Dr. Tanzio, wondering where Paul had gotten off to.

"He had a suitcase in his hand when he spoke to us, and then he got in his car and headed down the driveway." The other gardener added, hoping the doctor could fill them in on what was going on at the Castle. The doctor just nodded, and headed back the way he had come. When he walked back in, he noticed an envelope leaning against one of the silver candlesticks on the dining room table, addressed to Rita. He picked it up, and climbed back up the stairs with it in his hand.

"The gardeners said that Paul instructed them to ring the bells; he knew the sound of the bells would bring you back. He mentioned how you loved the sound of the bells at the convent, when you were a little girl. They said he took his bag and left. I found this letter addressed to you down on the dining room table, leaning against one of the candlesticks." Dr. Tanzio handed the letter to Rita, and she opened it up, pulling out the single sheet of paper inside.

"My Darling Rita,

I hope you can forgive me; the jealousy poisoned my soul and overwhelmed me, turning my heart to stone. I will spend the rest of my life regretting how I have treated you, you who were always the best part of me. Thankfully I woke up, before it was too late. I have never truly loved anyone but you, and you will always be the most important person in the world to me. I am happy you have found someone to love, and it is my hope that you and Renato will have a long and happy life together. I am turning the Estate and the Titles over to you, since

you are the most worthy and noble member of our family. You understand what it takes to care for this ancient and honorable place, the way my father and your father did.

I am returning to Switzerland to try and make some kind of a life for myself. I know Dr. Muller will welcome me to the staff of the University, and I will be staying with my aunt and uncle until I get settled. I will contact my lawyers when I get there, and instruct them to take care of all of the necessary legal paperwork. I intend for you a free woman, and the sole heir of our Title and lands.

I know you will breathe life back into the gardens, and make them bloom like Uncle Guido, who tended them with such loving care. The farms and the livestock will flourish like never before, and our produce will fill the market faire. There has been a dark cloud over this place for far too long, and I am confident you will return it to the Eden it once was. I will cherish my memories of growing up here with you, and hope your memory will fade of our misguided attempt to make our families happy. We should have realized that they already were

happy, and they only wanted us to be happy too. I am the loving brother I have always been to you, and it is my prayer that you will remember me that way.

Be well, I love you with all of my heart, Paul.

Rita bowed her head, and wept the tears of pure joy that her brother had indeed been restored to her. It had not been a dream. She would do as he had requested, and make Lake Braies the fairytale castle she had seen, driving up to the grand manor for the first time. She was lucky to have earned the love of two good men, and she would work hard to be a credit to both of them.

With that, the demon that had sought to steal the happiness of a proud and noble family slunk off into the shadows. He had been defeated, and would head to some dark familiar corner, to lick his wounds and wait. Happiness had won the victory today, but he was patient and would eventually find another opportunity to ply his trade. Everything had its opposite, and happiness could not exist if there were no sorrow. Somewhere there was a heart who would allow him to plant the seeds of greed and anger and jealously again. There would always be another day, and eventually he would recognize and seize the chance to come forth. He would save his strength and conserve his power against that hoped for day, turning to rend the person who was foolish enough to give him life.

I looked at the beautiful Castle across the lake, and wondered just how much of my Grandfather's tales were true. Grandpa had always spoken as if he had actually known the people he had filled my head with, as I played in the Tailor shop, under his great cutting table so long ago. Perhaps he had known them, or perhaps he had just heard about them, and filled in the rest of the story with his wonderful imagination. I loved this place that I had grown up in, a lifetime ago. I hope I can honor the memory of my family, by keeping the stories from my childhood alive.

The mountains and the town and the brave men who had fought and died here, they were all part of the fabric of my life. It was now time for me to go down the mountain, and face my own demon, the one who had lulled me into believing the lie of tomorrow. There is no tomorrow, there is only today. We should remember that, and make sure that we take care of the things that are truly important in our lives, and let lesser things take care of themselves.

This book was printed in Georgia typeface, with accents in Daniel, Gabriola, Palace Script MT, and Vladimir Script.

CPSIA information can be obtained at www.ICGtesting.com
Printed in the USA
BVOW08s2050230614

357176BV00005B/13/P